Effortless Divorce: Your Ultimate Step-by-Step Solution

Dewey .A Rowland

All rights reserved.

Copyright © 2024 Dewey .A Rowland

Effortless Divorce: Your Ultimate Step-by-Step Solution : Divorce Made Easy: A Simple Guide to Ending Your Marriage Painlessly.

Funny helpful tips:

Invest in employee well-being; a motivated team boosts productivity.

Practice speed reading techniques; they can enhance your reading rate without compromising comprehension.

<u>Life advices:</u>

Maintain robust data analytics; insights drive informed decisions.

Maintain a robust feedback mechanism; continuous improvement is key.

Introduction

This is a comprehensive guide designed to provide individuals going through a divorce with the necessary tools and guidance to navigate the emotional, physical, and spiritual aspects of the process. This guide aims to empower individuals to achieve freedom and find healing in various areas of their lives.

The guide begins by addressing the emotional aspect of divorce. It explores common emotions experienced during this challenging time, such as fear, worry, anger, resentment, blame, hurt, and grief. It provides insights and strategies for coping with these emotions and achieving emotional freedom. The guide also addresses sensitive issues like violence, abuse, substance abuse, and infidelity, offering support and guidance for those dealing with these situations.

Next, the guide delves into the physical aspects of divorce. It provides information and knowledge on various legal matters, including attorneys, property division, alimony, child support, and other relevant issues. It walks individuals through the divorce procedure, covering topics such as injunctions, discovery, negotiation, mediation, and trial. Additionally, the guide highlights the importance of estate planning and financial planning during and after divorce.

In the pursuit of spiritual freedom, the guide explores key aspects such as forgiveness, laughter, declaration, integrity, passion, power, and ultimately embracing a sense of freedom. It emphasizes the importance of finding inner strength and connecting with one's spirituality as a source of healing and growth during the divorce process.

Throughout the guide, step-by-step instructions and practical advice are provided to assist individuals in their journey towards achieving emotional, physical, and spiritual freedom. It encourages individuals to prioritize self-care, seek professional support when needed, and make informed decisions that align with their values and goals.

By addressing the emotional, physical, and spiritual dimensions of divorce, this book provides a comprehensive roadmap for individuals navigating the complexities of divorce. It empowers individuals to heal, grow, and create a new chapter in their lives with a sense of freedom, resilience, and hope.

Contents

EMOTIONAL FREEDOM	1
FEAR	2
WORRY	8
CONTROL	11
ANGER	18
RESENTMENT	22
BLAME	28
HURT	34
VIOLENCE	38
ABUSE	42
SUBSTANCE ABUSE	45
INFIDELITY	49
STORY	53
SELF-ESTEEM	58
SACRIFICE	62
GRASPING	66
GUILT	70
GRIEF	75
APATHY	79
RESIGNATION	83
DIGNITY	86
Physical FREEDOM	89
KNOWLEDGE	90
ATTORNEYS	94

LAW	98
PROPERTY	102
ALIMONY	108
PARENTING PLAN	112
CHILD SUPPORT	117
OTHER ISSUES	122
PROCEDURE	126
INJUNCTIONS	132
DISCOVERY	137
FACEBOOK	143
NEGOTIATION	147
MEDIATION	151
TRIAL	155
ESTATE PLANNING	160
FINANCIAL PLANNING	164
HEALTH	170
Spiritual FREEDOM	175
FORGIVENESS	176
LAUGHTER	180
DECLARATION	184
INTEGRITY	189
PASSION	193
POWER	198
FREE	203

Section One

EMOTIONAL FREEDOM

Day 1

FEAR

Fear! The word alone is frightful. The journey starts with fear for everyone. Universally, this is the first emotion expressed by clients during our first meeting. Each story is different and each is expressed in as many different ways as there are people. Maybe your word for it is "terror" or "fright" or "dread" or "worry" or "consternation" or "afraid" or "scared." However you say it, the sentiment is the same.

The definition of fear, according to the Merriam-Webster Dictionary, is: **1. a.** an unpleasant, often strong, emotion caused by anticipation or awareness of danger **b** (1): an instance of this emotion (2): a state marked by this emotion **2.** anxious concern. Living in fear affects every aspect of our beings—mentally, physical and spiritually. The kind of fear that we conjure in a divorce setting takes prisoners and is a ruthless captor, inflicting torture tactics that would make penitentiary wardens look like kindergarten teachers.

The time leading up to and during the divorce is brimming with fear. What is there to fear in your mind? The fears that I hear regularly are along the lines of this:

Fear of affording the divorce

Fear of the unknown

Fear of losing the kids or not seeing them enough

Fear of having to pay alimony

Fear of losing assets

Fear of what people are going to think if you get divorced

Fear of kids being angry at you for leaving the other spouse

Fear of retribution

Fear of impact on business

Fear that you'll gain a reputation that people might think you are hard to get along with

Fear of being talked about (gossip)

Fear of splitting up friendships

Fear of change

Fear of lifestyle change

Fear that kids might be disappointed in you

Fear of own relationship with self (Can I trust my own decision making process?)

Fear of being alone (Is there somebody out there that's really better? Do I want to be in another relationship? Will I ever marry again? Will I be lonely?)

Fear that you are being silly (He/she doesn't cheat on me, so he/she is a good person.)

Fear that you are being unreasonable

Fear that there is something "wrong" with you

Fear that you can't make it on your own

Fear that you won't have sex again, or for a very long time

Fear the other party will have the upper-hand in the divorce

Fear the other party is getting "more" of his or her "way" during the divorce

Scary, right? And this is by no means a complete and comprehensive list!

Consider FEAR as **F**alse **E**vidence **A**ppearing **R**eal. How does it appear for you? In your mind, fear is very real. How does it affect you? It paralyzes you, robs you of sleep, and steals your precious peace of mind. It often controls you like a marionette on a string, telling you to avoid conflict, avoid feeling your emotions. Often, it affects you physically, causing ulcers, headaches, cramps, nausea, depression, hair loss, hives or rashes. It is not a pretty sight.

What does fear motivate us to do—or not do? In my practice, I often see men and women who are very powerful and accomplished in their professional lives who, by contrast, have completely lost who they are at their core in their personal lives. Their souls are lost in the thick of an emotional forest, and the finest search parties with specially-trained rescue dogs would have trouble locating them.

Take, for example, Melissa, an accomplished physician who married late, and didn't want to admit her marriage was a failure. Having attended Ivy League schools and besting her colleagues by being selected as chief resident, she was chief of cardiology at a local hospital by the time she landed in my office. Now in her early 50s, she married a man 10 years her junior, and the marriage (so far) had endured just three short years. Her prince charming? Well, it turned out that he had several aliases and a history of engaging in fraudulent activity. He would disappear for long periods, and she had already given him thousands of dollars by the time I met her. Does it sound obvious to you that she should leave? Well, her take was not the same.

She still didn't want a divorce. Her parents were urging her to leave her husband, and I got the sense that she was sitting across from me to appease her parents. Yet, deep down, she knew that she deserved better. What fear held her captive in that relationship? Fear of being alone? Fear of being viewed a failure? Fear that if this man didn't want her, no other man would either?

When I reminded her how empowered she truly was and pointed out her accomplishments, she started crying. She said that she once was, but that she needed to go back and find that person. I never saw her again and, as far as I know, she is still married to that guy.

She may have chosen to stay in a relationship that was clearly not healthy for her. Choosing inaction is still a choice. What is the impact to her? A loss of the possibility of an authentic relationship to be sure, but the loss of her soul, and of the self that she could declare for herself, is an even greater loss. Her fear has frozen her in a place of unhappiness.

Lee Ann, a mother of two teenage daughters, had a deadbeat ex-husband who hadn't paid child support in years. He had remarried and had children with his new wife. While he could afford a new home and new cars, he apparently didn't leave enough room in his budget for the children he sired with Lee Ann. That being the case, Lee Ann was fraught. She was gripped with fear about taking her ex-hubby back to court to hold him accountable for his obligations.

Why? Well, she didn't want the children to be mad at her because she would be going after dad for child support arrears. She was nervous that her kids would be mad at her or shun her and take their dad's side, among a myriad of other fears.

Again, Lee Ann chose to do nothing. Instead, she resigned herself to harboring resentment and anger. This is the obvious repercussion. What are other hidden repercussions? One is that she is teaching her daughters that it is better to avoid conflict than to hold people accountable for their obligations. This situation reeks from a lack of integrity. Husband agreed to pay a certain amount in child support, then didn't bother to pay it. Wife agreed to take that amount in order to properly care for her children, then won't enforce the obligation. No amount of Lysol can clean up this mess.

Fear is a function of the ego, as the self feels threatened. Your soul and your spirit know that nothing can threaten the real you. The way to combat fear is to recognize it for what it is, look at it and call it out. Another way to combat fear is to arm yourself with knowledge, which I am providing you in this book. Only then will you be able to transform your fear into confidence and courage. When you face fear head-on and break through it, you feel empowered, inspired and strong.

Day 1 Exercise

1. Take a piece of paper and fold it into thirds.
2. On the first section of the paper, write down all of your worst fears.
3. On the second section of the paper, write down how you would like everything to be, as if you get to script your own life (and you can, but we'll get to that).
4. On the last section of the paper, write down what is real. What has actually happened and nothing more.

Day 1 Meditation/Affirmation

Close your eyes and breathe deeply. As you breathe in, imagine you are bringing in courage and strength. As you exhale, imagine that you are releasing all of your fears. Say to yourself, "I am courageous, strong and confident."

Day 2

WORRY

A *few years ago,* I learned a powerful lesson about the impact of worry in our lives. Amidst a sea of faces, and programs being used as fans, we made our way to our seats for my son's graduation from high school. The program seemed interminable as we waited for the few seconds that we got to cheer and capture any photographs we could while he walked across the stage when his name was called. It was uncomfortably warm and, despite the fact that he attended a relatively small, private school, the auditorium was packed to the brim. Many times in our lives, wisdom comes to us when we are least expecting it, and such was the case for me on this sultry May afternoon. At some point, which seemed like several hours into the ceremony, the valedictorian took her place at the podium, and the 18-year-old girl opened her speech with a statement that I have never forgotten. "The two biggest wastes of time are worrying and complaining," she said. Though I remember little else of what she said, I have often reminded myself of that gem of insight.

Heather is a good example of the debilitating and destructive power of worrying. She had moved to Florida from Indiana for a boyfriend, who she ultimately married after giving birth to a daughter.

When the child was two years old, the marriage went south, so she wanted to head back up North to be with her family. She was worried, constantly fraught with unanswered questions. She wondered whether she would be able to move, how long the case would take, and whether she would be able to appeal if she lost. This worry began to take its toll on her physically. She wasn't eating or sleeping properly, and began getting sick because her immune system had become weakened. Her husband had convinced her during the marriage that he could manipulate any situation his way and that any attempts to go against him would fail. Her doctor eventually prescribed Lexapro to help ease her anxiety, and she began seeing a therapist.

What is worry? It is a thought about what may happen. It has no basis in what is actually happening right now. If you look back on your life, how many times did you worry about something, only to find out that you had no reason to worry about it? The Merriam-Webster Dictionary defines worry as "to move, proceed, or progress by unceasing or difficult effort" and "to feel or experience concern or anxiety."

Worry does nothing for you. Worry is like that moocher houseguest. It accomplishes nothing, adds no value, and takes from you. Don't let negative thoughts live rent-free in your mind. They sap your energy and rob you of the joy of this moment because you are worried about what may or may not happen in the future.

Day 2 Exercise

1. Concentrate on what you are worrying about. Realize that worries are merely thoughts and resulting bodily sensations.
2. Visualize those thoughts as if they are taking up space in the room right in front of you.
3. Look at the thoughts, and tell them that you are setting them aside because they don't actually exist. They aren't real.

Day 2 Meditation/Affirmation

As you go through the day today, when your thought turns into worry, say to yourself, "This is just my body having these sensations, and these are just thoughts. You are not real and I am setting you aside."

Day 3

CONTROL

In divorce law practice, it is commonplace to hear one spouse accuse the other of being a "control freak." If one is the control freak, is the other one the victim, the one being controlled? If they are both control freaks, then disaster strikes—fires, explosions and the like. In order to be controlling, there has to be a willing participant who is being controlled. If one party is deeply fearful, often the natural response is to try to gain control of the situation and thereby (hopefully) minimize the fear.

The Oxford Dictionary defines control as "the power to influence or direct people's behavior or the course of events." In his book, *The Celestine Prophecy,* author James Redfield describes four distinct personalities, all of which are types of controllers. They are the: Interrogator, Intimidator, Aloof One and Poor Me. While some of these are overtly controlling and others choose stealthier, more covert methods, they share a common denominator in that the person has developed a way they each think they can manipulate others into doing what they want them to do.

INTERROGATOR

The Interrogator is constantly questioning the other person. In marriages, it may surface like this: Bob was married to Sue for 21 years. Bob was a physician who had invented a few medical devices, which afforded the couple a very comfortable lifestyle. They had three homes and traveled extensively. More of a proverbial wallflower, Sue allowed Bob to dictate and choose most of their activities throughout the day, as well as control the finances and other major decisions in their lives. During the marriage, he became increasingly suspicious of everything she wanted to do. He would question her about what she was wearing, and accuse her of trying to attract men. Now, mind you, Sue, while a nice-looking woman, was in her 60s, and kept her short-cropped hair silver. With her glasses, minimal makeup and conservative clothing, she could almost pass for a nun (because nowadays nuns rarely wear the full habit of yore). He became so suspicious that he would question how long it took her to run to the supermarket for groceries. The questioning of not only who she spoke to in a given day, but also why and for how long, was one of the many reasons why she finally had had enough and snuck her way into my office. She paid for the initial consultation in cash, of course. While the Interrogator doesn't bother to conceal his or her methods of attempted control, the one being interrogated feels compelled to take cover.

INTIMIDATOR

Scarier yet is the Intimidator. This perpetrator of control uses threats of violence or actual violence to bully people into getting their way. Stacey was a young girl in her 20s who had been married for three years too long by the time she first met with me. At that point, she said she was "thinking" about getting a divorce. As I always do, I asked what was going on. She said, sort of nonchalantly, that he had been a "little" abusive. "In what way?" I asked. Well, she said, he got physically violent during their honeymoon by pushing her around in the resort parking lot. (Note to anyone being physically abused by a spouse or significant other: It's time to get out. Right now. Pack your things and move on. Do not look back. Abusers need professional help and you don't need to stick around to see whether they get it or whether they are capable of being rehabilitated.) Meanwhile, she stayed three more years, and endured jaw-dropping means of force, which included a harrowing episode of attempted strangulation, which worked for him up until that point.

That the Interrogator and the Intimidator both try to use force as their chosen method of control is not the only thing they have in common. Both also resort to other means to facilitate their drive to make people feel humiliated, such as hurtling derogatory names and insults, degrading looks and generalized condescension. These are the bullies of our world.

ALOOF ONE

Then there are the passive-aggressive controllers: the "victims." The first one is the Aloof One. This one shuts down and won't let you in. Speaking in vague terms, this person's strategy is to make the other party in the relationship do all of the communicating, while remaining disconnected. This one often pairs well (I say this sarcastically but they do often find their way to each other) with the Interrogator. After being interrogated for a long period of time, this person sometimes implements the broad-brush approach to answering questions. The Aloof One doesn't ask much and doesn't tell much either, as if to say, "You stay out of my world and I am happy to stay out of yours." This drives the Interrogator, who must know all details, absolutely batty.

Here's a good example. Robin was married for 18 years to her husband, Steve. After 12 years of marriage, Steve decided he no longer wanted to work. Working several jobs to keep a roof over their heads, Robin supported them and paid all of their bills for six years. Steve, on the other hand, had become accustomed to a lifestyle in which he sat on the couch, watching daytime television, while Robin was out "bringing home the bacon and frying it up in the pan." (She cleaned the pans, too). In exchange for this lifestyle, for years, she endured his insults, put-downs and abusive behavior. He told her that she was fat, ugly and stupid; that no one else would want her; and that she was lucky that he still put up with her. Robin eventually grew tired of this joyless life that was going nowhere and decided she was ready to rid herself of Steve, who had become her albatross. Steve played the part of an Interrogator/Intimidator (yes, there can be this hellish combination) and would have no part of that. Completely satisfied with how things were, Steve was not interested in going along with her plan for a divorce. So, in response, he unleashed his "Super Interrogator/Intimidator" personality. He declared it a war and said if she didn't continue to pay the bills and stay married to him, that he would make her life a living hell. She politely thought about it and said, "Mmm, no." He became a nightmare. He was smoking in the house, eating her food, turning the thermostat down to 60 degrees, leaving the refrigerator and freezer doors open, and engaging in a multitude of activities directed at making her uncomfortable and annoyed. The more he engaged in these behaviors, the less she said to him. She would simply close the refrigerator doors, turn the thermostat back up, and didn't speak to him. By being the Aloof One, she didn't give him the satisfaction of feeling like he was controlling her. She also was trying to control him by acting this way.

POOR ME

The other furtive type of controller is the Poor Me. This one may be the most difficult to spot. Those who have perfected this strain of control have you in a proverbial chokehold that you didn't see coming. Here, the person makes you feel sorry for them and even guilty for not taking care of them enough, properly, or at all.

Health issues can be one avenue for this type of control. Blake was married to Elena for four years. Prior to the marriage, she had some back issues. During their marriage, she developed issues with asthma as well. Worse than a Grateful Dead groupie, doing the tour of the physician specialists each month became her hobby. Her tour stops included time with the back specialist and the pain specialist, then the pulmonary specialist and back to her internal medicine physician. She insisted on being pushed in a wheelchair when she and Blake were going out in public if the excursion would require more than 10 minutes of walking. At the time of filing the petition for dissolution of marriage, she requested permanent alimony. These are payments made by the husband to the wife until either of them die or remarry. However, Elena was not as debilitated as she acted. Elena was a singer in a local band. When it suited her, she could power up and sing her way through a two-hour concert. She was looking to manipulate both her husband and the court into a retirement plan for the rest of her life. All this for a mere four years of marriage? Try finding that deal from any employer. While her Poor Me act failed miserably with the court, it worked well on her husband for a period of time, and probably continues to work with others.

Manipulation and control aren't always necessarily negative. We all try to control or manipulate people in one way or another. At times, we try to get people to do what we want through flattery or incentivizing them in some way. We even appease our own egos by telling ourselves it is for the other person's own good.

In negative situations, however, it can become about domination vs. avoiding domination. This is where it becomes unhealthy and where there is no easy outcome. One wants to dominate the other one at any cost, and the other will avoid being dominated at any cost. One wants power and the other won't give it to them.

Control is really about fear. Knowing that you are whole and complete just as you are will allow you to let go of your need to control. It will also give you the courage to realize that no one has the power to control you but you. The most powerful people are those who feel no need to control others by force, nor are they controlled by others. Gandhi moved millions of people by living his truth and being confident in his self-expression. There is no difference between Gandhi and you. You can also live your life as the self-assured powerful expression of who you were created to be.

Day 3 Exercise

Write out your answers to the following questions:

1. What are you being right about that you could give up? Who are you making wrong? How are you justifying being right?
2. What are you actually winning?
3. What is it costing you to hold on to whatever it is that you're holding on to?
4. What are some ways in which you can let go of what, or who, you are attempting to control?
5. Write a description of what you look like as whole and complete. Who is that person? How does that person interact with others and the world? Spend the day focusing on being that person.

Day 3 Meditation/Affirmation

Today, tell yourself, "I can only control my own actions, feelings and emotions. I am whole and complete and will interact with others as though they are whole and complete."

Day 4

ANGER

*J*ust as cigarette packages have prominent warning labels on them, so should anger in the context of a divorce. The label might say something like "Danger: Anger in divorce may cause harm to you, your children and your loved ones, and may make you sick. Quitting now may reduce serious risks to your health!" While people who are experiencing divorce often go through the full gamut of emotions, anger may be the most toxic. In order to truly be free and ready to embrace your new life, letting go of the anger must be your starting point.

Divorce can bring out the worst in people and anger shows up in divorce in innumerable ways. Under the guise of "doing what's best for the children," anger causes people to use their children as pawns. Spouses cut off credit cards, embarrass the other one in public, and attempt to humiliate the other by exposing personal details. There are many other creative ways that an angry, bitter spouse attempts to cause the other spouse headache and heartache.

Here's a prime example of how it can spiral out of control. Bruce and his wife, Logan, met while he was in business school. She was a risk-taker who was willing to do anything for fun, and he loved her crazy energy. Together they started a technology business. She became the office manager and he directed the firm's development and performed the substantive work for their clients. The timing just right, the business took off, and within five years, they were earning millions of dollars. They also had three children along the way. By day, they seemed like a mild-mannered couple running their business together. During off hours, however, they were still wild and loose. In their world, that meant an open marriage in which they both had other partners, separately and together. They enjoyed recreational drugs such as marijuana and cocaine. They also built three multimillion dollar homes, traveled the world, and placed their children in the most expensive private schools.

During the marriage, they had huge knock-down, drag-out fights, but always managed to stay together and get back to taking care of business, professionally and personally. That is, until Logan met another man, who we'll call Chance, who was richer and better looking than Bruce. One day, she came home and told Bruce their marriage was done, packed her bags and moved into an even bigger mansion with Chance. Logan served Bruce with divorce papers.

Bruce, crushed at first, began surfing the Internet and quickly reconnected with an old flame through Facebook. They began corresponding. He eventually flew her in to visit him, they discovered that the flame still flickered, and they rekindled a relationship.

In the meantime, across town, after just a few months, Chance had already had enough of Logan, and requested that she remove herself from his bigger, better mansion. With nowhere else to go, she predictably decided that maybe life with Bruce wasn't so bad after all, and began her campaign to get him back. By then, he was no longer interested in her. And so began World War III.

Logan, enraged that Bruce wouldn't take her back, launched her campaign to destroy him. Bruce, incensed that she took her final bow and now wanted an encore, began his crusade to annihilate Logan. This manifested itself in a variety of creative ways. She filed a false domestic violence action against him, then he called the local child services department and filed a report that she was abusing the children. She broke into his house and super-glued appliances and other kitchen items to the counters. He called the landscapers and paid them to remove all of the landscaping from the home in which Logan was living. (It was still co-owned by him, so he had the authority to do that.) As her pièce de résistance, Logan contacted the Internal Revenue Service to inform them of his historically questionable business practices.

This cycle of rage and anger will not stop unless someone or something (usually traumatic or destructive) puts a stop to it. Remember the movie *The War of the Roses*? When you exact revenge upon another person, you are actually hurting yourself more than you are hurting the other person. While each action at the time seems satisfying, at its core it is very disempowering. You are giving power to the other person. In effect, you are saying, "You have power over my life and I am going to try to take away that power by exerting power over you." In reality, the other person only has the power you gave them. You don't think that a stranger you pass on the street has power over you. Nor do you think your kitchen table does or your hairbrush. While those last examples may seem absurd, they are offered to prove a point. There is an awesome source of strength in coming to the realization that you have given permission to the other person to have power over you—and you can revoke that power.

Anger is always a reaction to being hurt, to having your heart broken. Anger is a normal reaction. Often I tell my clients that they have every right to be angry. The danger lies in dwelling on the anger. You have a choice to hold on to your anger or to let it go. By letting go of the anger, you are not letting the other person "get away" with anything. The person who feels the most effect from your anger is YOU—not the other person. By letting it go today, you make a choice to take control of your own life and declare that you will have peace in your life.

Day 4 Exercise

Take a moment to sharply focus on the things that the other person is doing that make you angry, and figure out why they have that effect on you. Write a letter to the person and outline all of it. Be specific about what that person did or did not do that has made you angry. Then detail what the effect has been on you. Make sure you are really precise about that. Now go back and re-read the letter, with a particular focus on the part where you describe the effect your anger has had on you. Last, take the letter and tear it into the smallest pieces possible and throw it all into the trash. Your anger is now gone.

Day 4 Meditation/Affirmation

When you feel anger today, acknowledge it and tell yourself, "I am aware of my anger and am grateful for the lessons I am learning. I notice the anger's grip loosening its stranglehold over me." You will begin to feel much lighter and notice how much easier it is to breathe relaxingly.

Day 5

RESENTMENT

Anger's first cousin is resentment. Very self-righteous and judgmental, resentment is the judge and jury, declaring that "I am right and you are wrong." It is also very harmful, not to the person toward whom you feel resentful, but to *you*. In her novel *Crooked Little Heart*, Anne Lamott aptly describes resentment when she says it is like eating rat poison yourself and expecting the rat to die. Here are some of the other types of things resentment might say:

"If you weren't a cheater, I wouldn't have to leave you, so you owe me lots of money."

"If you weren't such a poor business person, we wouldn't have to sell our house."

"If you helped out around the house every once in a while, I wouldn't be so exhausted."

"If you made more money, we would be able to afford more, and I would be able to stay home with the kids."

"I am so grouchy because you are always off playing golf or tennis, and are never home to help me."

"You chose to cheat, and gave me a sexually transmitted disease, so you should pay dearly."

"I expected you to be my Prince Charming, but you take me for granted and haven't fulfilled my expectations."

"You were supposed to be my submissive wife who would take care of me, so how dare you have a career outside our home!"

"I am tired of dealing with your health problems and taking care of you. It is time for me to have a life for myself."

"I hate you and I'm going to get you."

"You are not communicating with me and I am tired of guessing what you are thinking."

"I may have cheated on you but that's because you withheld sex and you don't deserve anything from me."

Resentment might also be passive-aggressive: "You can't make me get a job or make more money. I don't have to do what you tell me, so I won't do anything." This type of resentment is not as overt, but just as insidious.

Merriam-Webster defines resentment as "a feeling of indignant displeasure or persistent ill will at something regarded as a wrong, insult or injury."

Resentment often wants exacting revenge. Larry, a vice-chairman of a Fortune 500 company, didn't particularly like conflict, and so when his marriage to Helen was very obviously nearing its end, he gave her what he thought was a generous offer, and was looking forward to an easy exit.

Helen, a self-described princess, fully intended to continue the lifestyle to which she had become accustomed. Throughout her life, she had made an excellent career of having various husbands support her, and ensured that she received generous settlements at the end of each marriage. (Larry was her fourth husband.) Still beautiful at 65 years of age, her breast augmentation was still holding up, her skin still smooth from her last face life, and her permanent makeup flawless. Nonetheless, realizing that she might not snag another rich husband quickly, she didn't want to take any chances. She wanted to receive every penny to which she felt she was entitled—and then some.

The reason for her burning resentment? Larry had spent some time in the company of other women. Helen felt betrayed and humiliated. She was embarrassed and believed that her socialite peers would look down on her. Driven by a lethal mix of anger, pride and resentment, Helen determinedly believed that the only antidote would be to make him pay alimony, and lots of it—for as long as they both continued to live.

The flip side to this equation is that Larry was riddled and wracked with inexplicable guilt. His guilty conscience was speaking loudly in his ear when he entered into a contract that required him to pay 72 percent of his gross income before his bonus, which was nearly 90 percent of his net income. While he was banking on a large bonus, that was never guaranteed. That decision may have been a salve for his guilt at the time, but within months, when the emotions settled and both of their new lives had begun, a new feeling surfaced in Larry: seething resentment. The circle of resentment was fully completed.

Resentment reverberates through the whole family. After 15 years of marriage and two children, Gianna and Simon were calling it quits. While he could be exquisitely charming, funny and intelligent, Simon also harbored a dark side. He could also be abusive, controlling and moody. Gianna, beautiful and successful in her own right, still loved Simon, but could no longer be married to him. Extricating herself from this relationship would require no less planning than an escape from Alcatraz.

Determined to move forward, she filed for divorce. Both equally competitive and stubborn, this move opened the floodgates to a battle for the children, who were only 8 and 6 years old. Each parenting plan was carefully scrutinized and the time with the children measured more precisely than timekeepers in the Olympics. If one was picking the children up at noon for a two-day visit, then the next pick-up time had to be precisely at noon. If one suggested 2 p.m. instead, then the other would have had two more hours with the children. Unacceptable. If he accompanied the children to a soccer game alone, then she wanted to go to the next game without him in attendance. And so it went. Pick. Pick. Pick. Pick. Pick. The holidays were even more of a disaster. They wanted to share Christmas Day —*equally*. Each day was precisely measured from the time the children arose in the morning to their bedtime. Of course, they each had to do a full Christmas dinner; one did it at noon and the other in the evening. The children had to endure two formal dinners. When Gianna showed up at a school event during Simon's parenting time, Simon clutched the children and wouldn't let them speak to their mother. Who were the real victims of this insane competition? Not Gianna nor Simon, but the children. They were stressed out.

The reasons for reducing your anger and resentment for your children's sake are very real. Studies have shown that children whose parents divorce amicably fare much better: They are healthier, become better students, and are more likely to be well-adjusted. Children of parents who have the most acrimonious divorces are more likely to run away, experiment with drugs, fall behind in school and get drawn into the wrong crowd.

Even more than your children, the direct victim of resentment and anger may surprise you. While you are fixated on your anger toward the person upon whom you place the blame for your emotions, the negative energy is harbored squarely in *you*. The impact is immediate and toxic. That negative poison courses through your veins and penetrates your cells. And it doesn't stop there. Like secondhand cigarette smoke, it adversely affects those around you. Because of your obsession, you can't enjoy the moments with your children or be present with your friends or your family. As a result, they, too, are sucked into the vortex of your bitterness.

Resentment accomplishes nothing, and the only person living with it 100 percent of the time is you. Therefore, let it go. Letting go of resentment usually involves forgiveness. Even if you are not ready to take the extra step to forgive, letting go of that resentment will allow you to create an open space that you can fill with joy, peace and relaxation. It's time to let the resentment go, and create that space of joy.

Day 5 Exercise

First, become present with your resentments. Write them all down in detail. Beginning first thing in the morning, find something to hold that fits in your hand. Imagine that object is all of your resentments. Carry this object around with you throughout the day and into the evening until you go to bed. *Do not* put it down for anything. Carry it with you to work, the gym, the grocery store, while you shower, walk the dog and eat your meals. No matter what your activity is for that day, make sure that the object is in your hand. Truly feel what it means to "carry" resentments and grudges. At the end of the day, when you put it down, feel the relief of ridding yourself of the object. When you release the object from your hand, feel yourself releasing your own resentments. Do not pick them back up again. Decide that you don't want to carry that extra burden with you anymore. Decide that from this point forward, you will choose what you want to have present in your life.

Day 5 Meditation/Affirmation

Affirm that, "Each moment of each day, I will be aware of letting go of my resentments and not carrying them with me. I am creating an open space where resentment once was, and am filling it with joy and contentment."

Day 6

BLAME

Years ago, when I decided that I wanted to leave a particular job, I dug up an old habit and pattern of thinking that I relied on to make major transitions. When I wanted something else, I had to make my current situation wrong. You know how that looks. Once you've decided to move on, practically everything about your current life looks wrong. You had never realized before how much you despised a particular aspect of the company or firm, how certain people's habits really bugged you, or how much a different department, policy or employee got on your nerves. While you're noticing this, you are subconsciously providing validation for your choice. While this transition is taking place, the voices in your head are telling you that you are making the right choice because the situation grows dimmer with each negative perspective or comment.

    The choice to end a marriage or a long-term relationship is never an easy one. Even if you have been separated for a long time, the relationship has been abusive, or you already have someone else, it is still a transition. With transition comes a flurry of mixed emotions: guilt, anger, resentment and the urge to want to place blame. When I wanted to end my first marriage, I had to tell myself (and everyone around me) that the reasons were numerous. I explained that we had grown apart; we wanted different goals; we got married too young (19 years old); we had too many children, too quickly, who were too close in age (three children in three years beginning when I was 20 years old). But the truth is that many marriages begin when the parties are young and children quickly arrive. They make it work and are happy together throughout their lives.

During my job transition, when I started back down my well-worn and comfortable path of laying blame on others around me to create reasons for leaving that position, a dear friend offered critical insight that forever changed the way I have looked at transitions. She said, "You do not have to make others wrong in order to make your choice right."

Why do we feel compelled to unleash weapons of mass destruction upon a person we once loved, upon a person who once was so right we made a commitment to be with them for a lifetime? What drives us to think that in order for us to feel any sort of satisfaction or peace that we have to inflict suffering upon the person, or color others' perspective of that person by making them seem less than human?

This is a completely different art of war. How does it manifest itself in divorce? In the business, we call it "scorched earth" litigation: You have fanned the flames of litigation so furtively that you have literally "scorched the earth" and there is nothing else to burn. The reality of this—aside from hundreds of thousands of dollars that go up in smoke—is that you cannot begin to heal. Continuing to file motion after motion, just to meet continued requests for filing motions and discovery from the other side, does not necessarily advance you closer to your end goal, which is to be divorced and to begin your new life. If your end goal is to make the other person suffer, then you must examine why that is. Take a hard look at what is lacking in yourself. What void you are trying to fill? Why does destroying the life of someone else, especially a person you once loved, give you pleasure?

This type of litigation must be distinguished from that of a divorce with dignity. The Latin root "dign" of the word dignity means "worth." With dignity, you can litigate (even aggressively) and still maintain a level of respect. Certainly this means respect for your soon-to-be ex-spouse, but also, and perhaps more importantly, respect for yourself. Define a level below which you won't stoop. Then have the integrity to stick to it. What does this look like? It is certainly appropriate to request the financial documents that are necessary to make an informed decision regarding a final monetary resolution of the case. It also may be entirely requisite for a parenting plan evaluator (a psychologist) to evaluate one or both parties in order to determine what is in the best interest of the children. Remember: Divorce with dignity does not mean that only one of you is left standing at the end of the process.

I have never seen a case in which a person who has engaged in trying to sabotage the other person's self-worth realizes any fruit from their wasted labor. This behavior typically generates more blame and resentment—all the way around. This kind of blame is like an insidious cancer—it spreads to your ex's support network, family, colleagues and lawyer. It can also spread to your lawyer when your legal fees begin mounting and you aren't getting what you want.

The temptation to engage in this type of battle may appear irresistible. The voices in your head may be playing much more loudly than the voices of your subconscious. They are telling you that you can't let him win; you can't let his lawyer win; you are doing this for the children; he deserves to suffer for what he put you through; she should get a job; or she doesn't deserve any of my hard-earned money. On and on the parade of destructive thoughts file through your mind, like waiting for an endless train to go by. Car after car of ideas goes by, each with a new way to wreak more havoc in the life of the other person.

What I know for certain is this: A crusade driven by blame is one that is destined for failure. The worst side effect of doling out revenge is that it doesn't truly affect the other person. Rather, it percolates into the depths of your own soul, and that damage may not be reparable. While your marriage may be irretrievably broken, your soul doesn't have to be too.

The world of blame is a "me against you" world, not a "me and you" world. It is one in which you are right and the other person is wrong. In reality, you are giving the person that you blame for your problems the power to control your world. If the other person is to blame then you are not. It's easier to fix blame for what we don't like about our lives, rather than working to correct issues and obstacles. What we don't like about our lives can range from big situations and experiences, such as your childhood, your career or your unhappy marriage, to more specific incidents, like who was at fault in a car accident.

The harsh reality is also your greatest revelation. You and you alone are the only one responsible for creating your own life and your own reality. Good or bad. No one else. By shifting the blame to someone else, you are actually giving control to that person. Without realizing it, you have declared that the other person has so much power over your life, he or she is responsible for where you are, how you feel or what your circumstances are.

Once you realize that you have no one to blame but yourself—and come to terms with the bare fact that you alone are in charge of creating your circumstances—you will feel an immediate sense of relief.

Day 6 Exercise

Throughout the day, notice how many times you find yourself blaming someone for something.

Each time you do, write it down in a journal or jot it down in the "notes" section on your smartphone so that no one else can see it. Your journal entries will look something like this:

"I blame my spouse for making me miserable because he was abusive." "I blame my spouse for my unhappiness because she cheated on me."

During your daily commute to the office or on errands, you might find yourself saying something like, "I blame that red Toyota for causing me to miss that light."

Each time you write something down, stop and ask yourself how you can take responsibility for your own feelings. Become aware of how you are giving the other person permission to dictate how you are feeling. Decide that you are going to rescind permission for giving them control over your life and take over control of your own emotions.

Day 6 Meditation/Affirmation

Today's thought is: "I am no longer giving anyone else permission to decide how I feel or dictate anything in my life. Only I have that power and I am using it to create a life I love."

Day 7

HURT

Anger, resentment and sadness are all reactions to being hurt, but many times we bury our feelings so deep that we don't recognize that. At other times, it is obvious that we are hurt, plain and simple. Hurt can result from a variety of sources. These are just some of the reasons why you might feel hurt:

Your spouse cheated on you.
Your spouse refuses to acknowledge your feelings.
Your spouse refuses to love your children from a different relationship.
Your spouse insults you, in private or in public.
Your spouse says that you are no longer attractive.
Your spouse won't acknowledge things that are important to you.
Your spouse shares emotional intimacy with someone other than you.
Your spouse does not want to spend quality time with you.
Your spouse does not help you with household duties.
Your spouse does not give you enough affection.

Layers of hurt can happen simultaneously. Phoebe was married to James, who was about 15 years her senior. It was a third marriage for both. They married when she was in her 50s and he was in his late 60s. He began to slow down due to medical issues. While being his nursemaid was not her first choice, she cared for him, and stayed by his bedside when he was hospitalized for several weeks.

Successful in business, James came to the marriage with more wealth than Phoebe, and he requested her to execute a prenuptial agreement. She reluctantly complied. One evening, several months after James had recuperated from his hospitalization, he solemnly directed Phoebe to pour a "stiff drink" and to sit down. He proceeded to tell her that he had deposited several million dollars in foreign bank accounts and that the Internal Revenue Service was on his tail. He claimed he had "forgotten" to report the income on those assets for several years. He then explained that Phoebe might also be mired in legal problems, too, because they had been filing joint tax returns throughout their marriage.

Phoebe was extremely hurt on two levels. The first was that he hadn't mentioned his offshore assets to her. She had worried about his health, remained at his bedside, cared for his needs, and lost sleep many nights as she worried about his medical issues and whether they would bankrupt them. She felt shocked and betrayed at this withholding of crucial information throughout the medical saga. Second, once he learned of his potential criminal liability, he hired the best attorneys for himself, but not for her. Brushing her aside, he told her that "she'd be fine." Using her own funds, she procured her own attorneys, and was able to gain a shield against IRS prosecution through the Innocent Spouse Relief program.

What no program could shield her from, however, was her deep sense of betrayal and profound hurt. What that hurt caused had the most impact. She began to distrust almost everybody, including her closest confidants who sincerely cared about her best interests. She began questioning her attorneys, her accountant and her neighbors.

The other impact was that she developed a grand sense of entitlement. She felt that she should be paid for her hurt. Had it not been for his behavior, she would have stayed in the marriage and would have still enjoyed some of his wealth. She wanted far more than what the law provided for her. The truth of the matter was that even if she had taken all of his wealth in a settlement, it would not have served as the salve she was seeking for her wounds. Hurting the other person in response to your own hurt doesn't provide relief or true satisfaction and never helps you to cultivate your own joy.

Relief will come in nurturing your own soul and realizing that there is a lesson in everything in our lives. If it were always sunny outside, we wouldn't appreciate the beautiful days. Rain serves a vital purpose in nature, just as the "rain" in our lives does. We don't learn from the easy times in our lives. The difficult times are the ones that give us an opportunity to grow and in doing so, breathes new life into us. So often, I tell my clients, "This will be the best thing that ever happened to you," and so often, they come back and tell me I was right.

Decide that the rain in your life is your blessing, and that you will learn valuable lessons from it. And remember: Above the rain clouds, it's always sunny.

Day 7 Exercise

1. Become present with the many reasons or ways that you may be feeling hurt. Write them down. Be specific and leave nothing out.
2. Think about the ways that hurt is impacting your life. How are you interacting with others because of it? What action or inaction are you taking in your life because of your hurt?
3. Write down the lessons you have learned from this hurt.

Day 7 Meditation/Affirmation

"I know the "rain" in my life is serving a vital purpose by allowing me to grow. I am looking forward to the sun and will appreciate it more each time it emerges from behind grey clouds."

Day 8

VIOLENCE

I am not going to mince words here. If you are attempting to control another human being through the use of physical force, please stop and seek help immediately. If you are living in a situation where you are being subjected to physical abuse (this includes pushing, shoving, slapping, hitting, kicking or any other sort of unwanted touching, including sexual), get out right now. Take your children and go to the nearest domestic violence shelter.

I know your excuses for not going—and here is what they basically are:

- I can't afford to live on my own and he or she is a good provider;

- He or she is really sorry afterwards and sometimes cries, and I always believe that it won't happen again;

- He or she is the father/mother of my children so I don't want to get them in trouble;

- I am embarrassed to let anyone know that I have allowed this to happen;

- No one in my family has ever been divorced, so I really want my marriage to work;

- It doesn't happen that often;

- It only happens when he or she has been drinking;

- I can help him or her change.

Listen and listen closely: All of these excuses are weak. You must put your safety first. It will happen again (and the level of violence can escalate). It is not okay. Abusers need professional help, but due to their controlling personalities and their denial of their inappropriate behavior, most don't seek counseling. This will not change and you should not be the one to help them. They have to want help first. Abusers are controlling bullies who only feel content or satisfied when exerting force over another. This is a frightening and debilitating way to live and is a wholly unacceptable environment for your sons or daughters. Whether you are the abuser or the abused, you are setting a terrible example for your children.

It is critical to understand that you didn't create this problem and it is not your fault. Acting differently, making a better dinner, having a cleaner house, or focusing on other external variables will not fix the problem. The problem is within the perpetrator, not the victim. You cannot fix the problem.

Create an escape plan. In addition to shelters, there are local support groups and hotlines, as well as websites, which can provide assistance and guidance. At a minimum, make sure you have access to cash and fuel in your automobile. Hide an extra set of keys if you can. Let a few people who are close to you know what's going on and memorize or store their contact information. Keep a small bag packed with necessities, including medications. Become familiar with the location of the nearest shelter. Rehearse your escape plan.

Always remember that you can call 911. A restraining order might also be warranted. If you decide to get a restraining order, try your best to hire an attorney who can help you draft the affidavit necessary for obtaining one. A good criminal attorney will know how to shape the events into a document that will pass muster under the statutory elements. This is what a judge will be looking for when determining whether to issue the restraining order. The attorney will also represent you at the hearing.

You deserve only the best for yourself and for your children. You also want your children to want the best for themselves. They don't need to grow up thinking that a violent relationship is normal or acceptable. Expect a life for yourself that you want for your children or for anyone you love.

Day 8 Exercise

Create an escape plan. Find out the telephone numbers of the local shelters and hotlines. Call the shelter and determine where it is located and what fleeing spouses can expect when they arrive. Identify a criminal attorney and a divorce attorney you might want to hire. Interview a few if you can—making sure to pay them in cash. Make it a priority to set aside some cash and hide an extra set of car keys that you can quickly grab. Pack a small bag with essentials in it and stash it somewhere that's easily accessible. Memorize or store the numbers for the shelter, your emergency contacts and other information you may want while in a shelter.

Day 8 Meditation/Affirmation

"I (or my children and I) deserve a safe and happy life."

Day 9

ABUSE

Just as detrimental, but perhaps not as obvious, are the hidden wounds that result from mental, verbal and emotional abuse. These kinds of injuries may even be more dangerous because they are not conspicuous, so the sufferer's need for help is not immediately recognized. Another form of control, mental and emotional abuse can take many forms, from constant criticism to outright name calling.

This is how one unhappy case developed. Penelope was a stunning girl from a tight-knit Midwestern family. Beautiful and smart, she had been a cheerleader and a homecoming queen who excelled academically. Her family—prestigious and well-connected in their community—made certain that she had every opportunity to succeed. Fresh out of college, she met Justin, a good-looking young man from a family with a sordid past, which included his father's federal conviction. Justin had two children with his first wife, unbeknownst to Penelope. But he pursued her relentlessly and finally won her heart (and the rest of her). They married and had a child.

The ink barely dry on the marriage license, he became controlling and verbally abusive. Having moved nearly 1,000 miles away from her family, he had free reign over her and he took full advantage. He began berating her on a regular basis, making her feel isolated, insecure and inferior to him. He insisted that she cook all meals, but constantly criticized her cooking. She couldn't seem to keep the house clean enough, establish a good schedule for their son, dress properly or comport herself to his standards. Prince Charming was really Prince Charmless.

With no history of divorce in her family, Penelope was determined to make the marriage work. She sought counseling and treatment, insisting in therapy that she could be a better wife and mother. Eventually, with the loving support of her family coupled with her fierce will to survive, she was able to realize what was happening and escaped the toxic situation.

These kinds of relationships tend to poison slowly, like arsenic. Victims are managing their daily affairs when they begin to notice that their relationship with their spouse has oddly evolved. But, there is laundry to do and kids to take care of, so the uncomfortable signs that things aren't right are swept under the rug. In the meantime, victims of verbal and emotional abuse work harder to please or appease the other spouse, by trying to cook better meals, make more money, or work more around the house. There is a concerted effort to respond to specific points of criticism with the hope that the relationship will improve. This is especially true for those who already have a low self-esteem or grew up being criticized.

If you feel like you are walking on eggshells when your spouse is around; like you can't express yourself because of the potential reaction; feel stress or dread when your spouse returns home from work, then you are in a verbally, emotionally or mentally abusive relationship. If your spouse does not respect you, or degrades, demoralizes or insults you, then you are in an abusive relationship. Physical abusers cannot stop themselves, and neither can emotional or mental abusers. Sometimes, people think their situation isn't so bad because they are not being physically injured. It is not okay. This type of abuse will have lasting repercussions on your mental and/or emotional state, as well as your children's, so exit the relationship as soon as you recognize the situation.

Day 9 Exercise

Demand the best for yourself. Know that you are worth it. The level of respect you will receive will be defined by the level of respect you have for yourself. If you think you are unlovable, you will not experience love. You have to be open to receive it. Journal what an ideal supportive partner would look like to you. Write out all of the characteristics that person would have if you could create that person. Decide that type of person is the only type you will accept into your life. If the person you are with does not meet your qualifications, make plans to clear that space so that the right person has room to come along. Reach out for help. Go to a therapist or join a support group. Lean on those who support you.

Day 9 Meditation/Affirmation

"I am a beautiful, lovable person who deserves respect."

Day 10

SUBSTANCE ABUSE

Deciding to leave your spouse under any circumstance can be distressing. Deciding to leave your spouse who has an addiction can be downright heart-wrenching. It often seems cold or cruel to think about leaving someone who clearly needs help. The hard truth is that an addict cannot be helped until the individual is ready and understands that they are powerless over their addiction. Living with an addict can be a nightmare and the thought of leaving an addict that you love can seem unthinkable. We instinctively want to help people we love to heal and get better. However, it is virtually impossible to help an addict who does not think there is a problem that's affecting their health, relationships and well-being. Any form of assistance becomes enabling, which is one of the worst things you can do for an addict. Forms of enabling include ignoring, making excuses for or rationalizing the behavior, believing that it's your fault, calling in sick for the person, financially supporting the addict, or bailing them out of jail and paying their legal fees—anything that creates the falsity that the addict's problem isn't so bad because they haven't hit bottom yet.

BOUNDARIES

Creating boundaries for yourself is an essential element for survival. It allows you to create a separation in your mind between your need to nurture and the addiction itself. If you don't make this separation, you will be burdened with guilt for not exercising your nurturing instinct. Remember that this is a disease and to treat the disease, it cannot be fed. At the very minimum, engage in "tough love" tactics and do not continue to enable the addiction.

LETTING GO

If your spouse is still being run by addiction and it's making your life miserable, you have to make a change. Only you can know when it is time to leave your spouse. While you are contemplating a move, think about its effects on you and your children, and what your default future will be if you don't make any changes. Assume that your addicted spouse will not change—and the situation will likely worsen. Simply assuming that your spouse might change will not help you now or in the long-term, and, quite frankly, it's not realistic.

Once you have decided to leave, be ready to follow through when you tell your spouse you are leaving. Threatening to leave and then staying is another form of enabling. Before you share your decision with your spouse, do your homework. Have a place to go and a plan in place. Get yourself emotionally prepared. Let your spouse know that you truly care but they need professional help, and that merely promising to get help won't change your mind. Remain strong and resolute in your decision.

Be prepared for the addict to get angry and blame the addiction on you. One of my clients had a husband who was a prominent resident in their community but had a serious drinking problem. She once found him passed out in the children's playroom, so inebriated that he was lying in his own urine. He awoke from his drunken stupor in a rage and attacked her. Afraid for her life, she called 911. When his picture and story appeared in the local newspaper, he lost his job. What happened next? Was this the soul-searching event that made him realize that he was powerless over alcohol and needed to get help? Unfortunately, no. He promptly blamed the mess on her. For a period, she believed it was her fault, lamenting that she had called 911, and wallowing in guilt. Eventually, she realized that it was his problem and not hers. She formed her escape plan, gathered her courage, and left the house. She has never looked back.

In Al-Anon (an anonymous support group for families and friends of addicts), the mantra is, "I didn't cause the addiction. I can't control it. And I can't cure it." Remember that. You might want to consider going to a local Al-Anon meeting. The meetings are free of charge and available at any time of the day, in every city in the United States.

Melanie Beatty writes in *The Language of Letting Go* that you can move forward with your life and your own recovery even though someone you love is not yet recovering. Choosing to live your life to the fullest does not have anything to do with the person who has not personally reached the decision to recover. It only means that you have the clarity and inspiration to move forward with new beginnings, and are choosing to live an empowered and healthy life.

Day 10 Exercise

Write out your answers to the following questions:

1. List five ways this person's addiction has affected your life.
2. List five ways that you have enabled this person's addiction.
3. List five ways that your, and your children's, life will be like if you don't leave.

If you have decided to leave, create a plan of action. Include a financial plan, a place to go and timeline in which you will be making it happen. Start to take steps to put the plan in place.

Day 10 Meditation/Affirmation

"I didn't cause the addiction. I can't control it and I can't cure it. Today I will begin living my own healthy and inspired life."

Day 11

INFIDELITY

For most people, few things are more devastating in life than to find out that you have a cheating spouse. In marriages that end in divorce, infidelity is one of the most oft-cited reasons for the demise of the relationship. The reasons people go "off the reservation" (as one of my clients aptly put it) are as numerous as the number of people cheating.
That said, here are a few of the common ones:
- My spouse doesn't like sex.
- My spouse doesn't want to do the kinds of things I want to do.
- We are basically separated anyway and no longer have a connection.
- My spouse puts me down, so it was great to feel attractive again.
- My spouse cheated first, so I felt like I could do it, too.
- I am no longer attracted to my spouse.
- It was payback for being mistreated or unappreciated.

Other reasons might be that the person has a sex addiction, or feels entitled and doesn't want to be controlled. Another reason I have heard lately is a reconnection to a long-lost love. Relating back to self-esteem and addiction issues, infidelity is most certainly a symptom of a deeper underlying issue. It is also a moral issue that can wreak havoc in your professional career. The public loves to be the judge and jury when given an opportunity; if you don't believe me, ask John Edwards.

According to data collected from The Normal Bar, 33 percent of men and 19 percent of women admitted to being unfaithful. Also interesting is the frequency of how often people said they cheated. Seventeen percent of the women who'd been sexually unfaithful and 23 percent of the men said it happened only once; and 36 percent of women and 33 percent of men said it happened two to five times. What this means is that more than 40 percent of unfaithful men and women admitted that they were regularly unfaithful. *(Copyright © 2013 by Chrisanna Northrup, Pepper Schwartz, and James Witte. Published by Harmony, an Imprint of the Crown Publishing Group, a division of Random House, Inc.)*

By the way, cheating is no longer limited to just physical sexual escapades. Books have been written on emotional affairs, which can be just as detrimental to a marriage. With the tidal wave of social media, this topic has roared into our lives and is here to stay for the duration. It is wise to beware of all forms of infidelity.

In the divorce setting, infidelity can mean absolutely nothing or it can mean everything. Many states have adopted a no-fault approach to divorce, meaning that infidelity is essentially irrelevant unless the cheating spouse has spent a lot of money on the other person, in which case the wronged spouse would be entitled to one-half of that amount. However. in states where grounds to divorce are still required, infidelity can play a starring role.

In divorce negotiations, even in no-fault states, the infidelity curse may continue to be present. Recently I handled a divorce for a former C-level executive who was a serial philanderer. He blamed his wandering ways on his wife, citing her lack of interest in sex. When his wife found out about his cheating, she also received the heartwarming news that he had given her herpes. A double dose of news. Though she was quite displeased, he was equally as contrite. He was deeply troubled by the idea of losing her and the many years of marriage they had shared. While he had apologized six ways to Sunday, she still didn't feel he had true remorse for his behavior. After listening to him, I started to see why. Every time he would express his remorse and regret to me, it was punctuated with the fact that she just didn't like sex. If I were his wife, I would think that he was trying to blame me for his infidelity in a backhanded way. This affected the negotiations because when it came time to mediate the case, her demands were stratospheric. She wanted him to hurt the way he had hurt her, and wanted him to be punished. He relented to her demands because he wanted to make amends with her and their children.

One of the ripple effects of this case was that she purposefully poisoned the children against their father. While she was filled with anger against him, her shortcoming was failing to create a shield between her hurt and the children's hurt. His wrong was toward her and not the children. Causing the children to feel disdain toward their parent only serves to create confusion and internal conflict in them. Regardless of how you feel, your children continue to be related to their parent. It is not fair or wise to place them in the crossfire of your pain.

The other side to cheating is the spouse who seems to have no remorse or guilt. I had a male client whose spouse cheated while she was pregnant with their second child. They had to perform a paternity test when the child was born to make certain the child was biologically the husband's child. Instead of being remorseful, she went after the husband for alimony and threatened to relocate with the children. She was projecting her anger onto him, creating upset around him to deflect the blame away from her. This also created a difficult climate in which to negotiate.

Infidelity is one of the three "Deadly Marriage Sins" (abuse, addiction and adultery). When the two of you become the three of you, it gets quite crowded in the marriage. Overcoming these issues of hurt and betrayal can seem insurmountable, and often times within the context of the marriage they are. If you and/or your spouse have determined that parting ways is the only solution, decide that this will be your moment of truth, your chance to choose to live in integrity going forward. The past cannot be changed, but the canvas of the future remains yet to be painted.

Day 11 Exercise

If you are caught cheating, don't deny it or blame it on your spouse. If you are the victim of a spouse who cheated, do not involve your children. Work on leaving the past as the past and determine how you plan to move forward. Are you going to try counseling? Make an appointment with a therapist. Are you going to get a divorce? Seek legal advice. Regardless of which side you end up on, let go of anger. Let go of having to be the one who is right and making the other one wrong. Let go of feeling like it's your fault. Move forward with a plan of action which is positive. Focus on the positive aspects of yourself and your partner. Even if you are moving forward with a divorce, concentrate on the positive. Positive energy will begin to heal your wounds and your soul.

Day 11 Meditation/Affirmation

"Today I am focusing on the positive aspects of my life and my spouse. This positive energy is healing me and allowing me to be whole."

Day 12

STORY

When I was in law school, I took an exceedingly boring class called Analysis of Evidence—an elective I chose because it fit in my schedule. To my surprise, I gained two valuable things from it. The first was my husband—we met in that class. The second was an interesting theory in law called "confabulation." As it was explained, confabulation consists of the stories that people concoct in order to fill in the gaps in their memories. In the legal arena, these are dangerous because lawyers often win cases with witness testimony, but the theory of confabulation can call into question the reliability of a witness's account.

And the truth is, humans are fantastic storytellers. A good friend of mine says that we are "meaning-making machines." From the moment we wake up and begin our day interacting with others, until we hit the bed at night, our imaginations run wild and control us, unfolding without our awareness. For example, you see someone you know and say hello. He or she responds coolly with a curt greeting. Your mind is off to the races: You begin to wonder whether you might have done something to offend the person. Or perhaps the person is arrogant or moody? Maybe the person doesn't like you. The list of possibilities that your mind can conjure is endless.

Speculation is dangerous because you begin to draw conclusions based upon the stories and assumptions you create, which doesn't necessarily equate with reality. After creating your own story, the next step is interacting with others as though your assumptions are true. In our example, the next time you see that person, you might give an unfriendly hello or perhaps ignore the person completely. You would never know that the person was simply having a bad day or was dealing with a personal crisis, and the curt response had nothing to do with you. However, because you have acted on your assumptions, you now have an interpersonal conflict with that person.

We tell stories all day long about how other people perceive us and about what other people's behavior means. In our example, look at what actually happened: You saw a person and said hello and that person also said hello to you. That is it. The rest was all a story.

We create our own suffering by the stories we choose to tell and believe. For example, women will often describe their husbands as abusive, and then they tell the same story to their friends, family and therapist. Let's say that what actually happened was that the husband asked the wife to stick to a budget, and the conversation resulted in name-calling. Describing it as abusive is the *characterization* of it. The husband might say that asking his wife to stick to a budget is critical for financial planning. Take another example. If you get angry with a motorist in a parking lot, and the driver calls you a bitch, your story will be that you were disrespected (but probably not that you were being greedy for trying to take a parking spot from a driver who was there first). Each person has a different story. It is in your characterization of the story that your personal suffering lies, because it shifts the true issue onto someone or something else. Rather than forcing you to explore where you can improve or grow as an individual, or to find the root cause of a major problem, you characterize the story.

If your spouse starts to cheat, you have the choice to tell the story that it happened because you are not worthy of your partner's love or because you are not young or attractive enough. The spouse's story may be that the cheating was the result of his sex addiction. The actual fact of what happened was that a person had sex with another person who was not a spouse. The meaning or cause behind most situations is what the storyteller brings to it—or how it is characterized.

Words are extremely powerful. In his book *The Four Agreements*, Don Miguel Ruiz explains the first "agreement" (to "be impeccable with your word") by pointing out that words are powerful tools with which we create our sentient world. Information, thoughts, concepts and emotions come to us in the form of language. The impact of our stories upon our psyche is paramount. Ruiz states it succinctly:

> "The word is the most powerful tool you have as a human; it is the tool of magic. But like a sword with two edges, your word can create the most beautiful dream, or your word can destroy everything around you. One edge is the misuse of the word, which creates a living hell. The other edge is the impeccability of the word, which will only create beauty, love, and heaven on earth. Depending upon how it is used, the word can set you free, or it can enslave you even more than you know. All the magic you possess is based on your word. Your word is pure magic, and misuse of your word is black magic."

In the context of divorce, it's especially important to be careful with your word and the stories you choose to tell. It is easy to veer off into the weeds, especially when your soon-to-be ex-spouse is telling stories about you that are not true. When that happens, the temptation to tell yourself stories about your spouse and others may become even greater. During the process of divorce, lawyers generalize that all husbands characterize their wives as "crazy" and all wives characterize their husbands as "abusive." This is quite an exaggeration, of course, but the impact of believing these stories causes continued and unnecessary suffering for each party.

By retelling the story that you are a victim, that you are unlovable because you've been rejected, or that your spouse is an egregious partner or parent, you get stuck. Like a scratched record that keeps playing the same part of a song over and over, your stories begin to wear a groove into your mind. You come to believe that they're actually true. Sometimes, you want to keep telling certain stories because it helps to assuage your guilt for wanting to leave the marriage. Sometimes, you keep telling the stories because you are seeking attention as a victim. Oftentimes, you don't even realize that your thoughts are just stories you have created.

What is certain is that these negative stories do not serve you in the long run. Eventually, your friends grow tired of feeling sorry for you and hearing the same stories. Eventually, these thoughts can affect your mood, your health and your well-being. While grasping negative stories is tempting, by choosing to use your words to tell a different, more positive story, you are choosing to elevate the level of energy in your life.

Breaking old patterns of thinking is not easy. In fact, it can be very difficult. Most of our thoughts are habitual and subconscious. We have to pay careful attention to our thoughts in order to determine what stories we are creating. Being aware of them is the first step toward breaking free from them. Only then can we begin the process of deliberately creating new thoughts to replace the old ones.

Day 12 Exercise

1. Notice what types of thoughts you have about each person with whom you interact today. Then answer the following questions:
    a. What do you think each person thinks of you?
    b. What do you think of each person?
    c. In your opinion, what was the meaning behind what they said?
    d. What do you think their body language means?
2. Go back to 1(c) and 1(d) and come up with three other possible meanings that have nothing to do with you.
3. Choose one of your new meanings from 2. The next time you interact with that person, communicate based on the assumption of one of your new meanings. Notice the difference.

Day 12 Meditation/Affirmation

"Today, I will tell only positive stories. If I don't like one of the stories, I will tell a different one. I will choose to use my words carefully, and in ways that are beneficial to me."

Day 13

SELF-ESTEEM

I *once read an article titled*, "Which Came First: Low Self-Esteem or the Divorce?" Harkening back to the old chicken-or-egg proposition, it is an interesting question. Most articles contemplate how to repair one's self-esteem after a divorce. The basic premise appears to be that the divorce might have been the direct cause of an ex-spouse's low self-esteem. One of my mentors, a gentlemanly divorce attorney, has often stated that in his 50 years of practice, he observed one common factor in every single divorce in which he was involved: One or both of the parties suffered from a lack of self-esteem.

In this age of talk shows, self-help books and websites galore, the notion of self-esteem is tossed about like popcorn in a movie theater. Merriam-Webster defines "self-esteem" as "a confidence and satisfaction with oneself; self-respect." Lack of self-esteem has a myriad of faces, all of them unpleasant. Some of the faces can be Mrs. Victim, Mr. Controller, Ms. Envy, Master Jealousy or Miss Bully. There are many others, none of whom you want to keep company with. Many times, you don't see these faces immediately. Billy Joel sings in *The Stranger*, "Well, we all have a face that we hide forever, and we take them out and show ourselves when everyone has gone." So, sometimes, we don't fully know a partner or lover until we have already married them.

Each of us is plagued with niggling insecurities. The danger is when insecurities grow into an unhealthy preoccupation or burden. Warning signs include thinking that you can "fix" someone else or harboring the impression that you "can be fixed" by a spouse or partner. We often believe that the other person will make us feel better, and romantic movies further that myth. Who can forget Tom Cruise's heart-stopping line in *Jerry Maguire*, "You complete me?" It may feel natural to become convinced that we are so valuable to our spouse that we actually "complete" him or her. But what happens when that person isn't around? Are you then not complete? This can't possibly make sense. The void you feel cannot be filled by anyone but you. You wouldn't want it any other way.

Jane Fonda eloquently observed, "We weren't meant to be perfect. We're meant to be whole." If you are looking at external forces to define yourself, you will always be disappointed. Nobody else should be given the power to define whether you consider yourself smart or beautiful or, more importantly, valuable. I have raised two daughters, and raising girls can sometimes be a particular challenge. One day, your daughter has a wonderful group of best friends, and the next day, those same friends have viciously turned on her. The news today is replete with stories of bullying that culminate in tragic suicides—young people filled with promise who've decided that their lives had no value because someone else said so. (Whether deliberate or inadvertent in their negative comments, the maligner was probably completely unaware that they had that much say, or power, over the other person.) When friends turned, I always asked my daughters, "Why are you allowing someone else to determine how you feel about yourself?" Give no other person the power to make you feel bad, or good, about who you are. If you are giving away this power, you will never be satisfied. The world is too iffy. Keep that power for yourself and yourself alone.

In *The Wizard of Oz*, Glinda the Good Witch tells Dorothy that she possessed what she was seeking all along, right there in her own heart. The beautiful thing about being secure in this knowledge is that you will become more valuable to yourself and to everyone else around you.

Day 13 Exercise

In the morning, take a piece of paper and draw a line down the middle of it. On the left side of the paper, write everything that you don't like about yourself. Across from each description—on the right side of the line—write the opposite description. For example, if you wrote "insecure" on the left side, then write "secure" on the right side. If you wrote "overweight" or "unattractive" on one side, then write "beautiful" or "attractive" on the other side. When you are done, tear or cut the paper in half, separating the right side from the left side. Take the left side, which contains your perceived negative attributes, and rip it up. As you do that, decide that that person no longer exists. The only person that exists is your new creation. Carry the positive list with you throughout the day. Look at it at least every hour to remind you of the new person you are.

Day 13 Meditation/Affirmation

Remind yourself throughout the day, "I love myself and respect myself. I am worthy, whole and confident. I deserve nothing less and will accept nothing less."

Day 14

SACRIFICE

Many years ago, Elton John crooned the poignant lyrics, "And it's no sacrifice, just a simple word. It's two hearts living in two separate worlds. But it's no sacrifice, no sacrifice, it's no sacrifice at all." This song, appropriately named *Sacrifice*, is a departure from most love songs: It proclaims the break-up of a marriage and declares that it is not a sacrifice because the partners have grown so far apart.

Compromise is expected and healthy in any relationship. What I submit is that sacrifice and compromise are not one in the same. Sacrifice is compromise's corrupt cousin. Compromise is a choice made within the realm of being whole and complete in order to keep the relationship flowing and fluid. Sacrifice takes a chunk from your soul and leaves you feeling like you are less or weakened in the process.

Take Susan, a talented concert pianist who had gone to college on a music scholarship and dreamt of touring the world. Instead, she met Brett when she was in her early 20s, and they married almost immediately. Together, Susan and Brett had decided early on that Brett should focus on his career as a rising corporate executive, and she would forego her own career aspirations, stay home and raise the family. They moved every few years. Now in their early 50s, Susan had had enough of the spotlight always shining on Brett and what she began to view as his selfish ways. She was ready to move on, but all she could focus on was the sacrifice she had made for Brett.

Susan's story is common. The notion that sacrifice is a positive virtue is more difficult for men to embrace than for women. Society expects women to sacrifice. Women are expected to put their children and husbands before themselves. That is not to say that men don't sacrifice. Men will often say that they relinquished their dreams of following their passion in order to keep a steady job to support the family. Sacrifice just shows up differently for each.

In a relationship, sacrifice isn't limited to career choices. You may sacrifice where you want to live, the lifestyle you want, the way you want to raise your children or run your finances, the kind of foods you want to eat or the kind of sex you desire. The list is truly endless!

But this is where another odious character enters the drama: in the form of the martyr. This is when you have decided that you have been the only one willing to sacrifice, so manipulating your spouse by playing the victim seems like a good strategy, and it may seem to work. By emphasizing what you have sacrificed—thereby making your spouse feel guilty and forcing them to do things you want them to do—you feel a small sense of vindication.

Unfortunately, there are some serious flaws in this scheme. First, neither of you will ever feel that this is a healthy relationship from which you receive a sense of long-term contentment or beneficial reciprocity. Secondly, and more importantly, it is not sustainable. Eventually, you will grow tired of playing that tune and your spouse's response will not feel like enough to sate you, or on the other hand, your spouse will grow tired of the guilt trip and decide to exit the drama.

I am going to be straight with you. You cannot change the past, and you must take responsibility for your own choices. You are where you are in your life right now as a result of choices you made. No one else's choices. Playing the martyr is a powerless role. You made the choice to marry young and have your husband take care of you. You made the choice of staying in the steady job to take care of your family instead of becoming a rock singer. The great news is that you still have choices. Create boundaries and decide where you want to compromise in your life and relationships and, perhaps most importantly, *where you don't*.

No longer a prisoner of sacrifice, you get to decide what your life will be, how it will look, and how it's going to happen.

Day 14 Exercise

Write down the following:

1. What sacrifices have I made for this relationship?
2. Why did I make them?
3. What other choices did I have at the time they were made?
4. What do I want my life to look like today?
5. What choices do I have today to do that?
6. What is stopping me?
7. How do I overcome what is stopping me?

Day 14 Meditation/Affirmation

"I will no longer make sacrifices. Today, I will decide what I want for my own life."

Day 15

GRASPING

"Why do you want to be with someone who doesn't want to be with you?"

I have lost count of how many times I have asked my clients this same question.

Recently, I had a meeting with Sheryl, who had been married for 30 years. In our first meeting, she proceeded to tell me in a matter-of-fact manner that her husband was an alcoholic and had a girlfriend, but she wanted to stay married to him. When I asked her why, without hesitation she replied, "Because we've been married for 30 years."

Grasping onto a relationship serves no one, least of all you. You may have lots of reasons why you are grasping, and they all sound plausible. The reasons might be:

I still love my spouse.

I don't believe in divorce.

We have been married a very long time.

I don't think I can make it on my own.

I don't want to be alone.

I don't want the stigma of divorce.

I want to stay together for the children.

Based in fear, the reasons for grasping onto the relationship are not rooted in healthy soil. Grasping is desperate. Grasping causes anxiety. There is no honor or dignity in being with someone who doesn't want to be with you, and there is neither honor nor dignity in being with someone you do not love. Perhaps greater still, there also is a lack of integrity. Each of you deserves to be with someone who thinks the sun rises and sets where you are. You also want to give your children a model of a loving relationship. You want them to want that for themselves. You don't want them to grow up and expect that merely tolerating one's partner is an acceptable way to live.

If you are grasping a relationship, it is essential that you look at the real reason for that. Often, it goes back to your own lack of self-esteem, lack of confidence, or the family models you were raised with. Holding that person hostage in the relationship will not improve these issues. In fact, it can make them worse. If you decide to stay, when your spouse has already stated they want to leave, a lack of self-esteem will fester into maniacal jealousy and distrust. You will constantly be on guard.

GRASPING DURING DIVORCE NEGOTIATIONS

Grasping also impacts you in the negotiation process. If you don't want to do anything that might affect a reconciliation, you could negatively compromise your settlement. Your spouse might know that, and use it as an advantage. Here's a prime example:

Desperate to save her marriage, Amy, during the litigation process, continued to communicate with Rick. I counseled her against it, but she would continue to talk to him about potential settlements in their divorce action. Meanwhile, he continued manipulating Amy in an attempt to get her to do what he wanted her to do. In this case, that meant settling for little or no alimony (which she was clearly entitled to) and an unfair property settlement (more of the assets went to him rather than to her, although she was entitled to more under the law). Her pattern, when he would become this way, was to retreat and feel intimidated. In reality, she didn't want the marriage to be over.

Our counseling continued but she was ready to cave into Rick's demands. One day, she began to question our case strategy and her decisions. I pulled her aside and said, "Look, you have three choices here: A) Stay in the marriage; B) Roll over and settle for exactly what he wants to give you; or C) Assert yourself and receive what you are entitled to under the law."

I went on to tell her, "You've had an intimate relationship with this man. You're dealing with someone who's had affairs and is hiding money. He has engaged in bad behavior and he is creating upset so he doesn't have to deal with his own lack of integrity."

That was a wake-up call for her. Amy chose option C and decided to assert herself. Ultimately, she got what she deserved under the law, and she found a wonderful man after the divorce. To this day, they are together in a healthy, fulfilling relationship. Amy could not have been ready for this relationship without building her self-confidence and self-esteem by standing up to Rick, overcoming her fears, and letting go of the ideals she held about her relationship with Rick.

Sometimes, when things seem like they are falling apart, they are actually falling into place.

Day 15 Exercise

Write down the following:

1. What are you grasping to?
2. What are your reasons for grasping?
3. What is the impact of this grasping on you?
4. What is the impact of clinging onto this relationship and others around you?
5. What is the worst thing that can happen if you let go?
6. What is the best thing that can happen if you let go?

Day 15 Meditation/Affirmation

"Today, I am letting go of feelings of desperation. I deserve someone who will love me and I will find that person."

Day 16

GUILT

Carla knew that her husband was a good man and a good provider who was dependable and a loving dad. She simply didn't love him anymore. She wanted a divorce. The guilt was nearly unbearable.

Mitch was a sex addict married to his high-school sweetheart. Conducting a double life for years, he was seemingly a model husband and family man. The guilt he harbored about his clandestine activities caused him to be hospitalized due to a nervous breakdown.

Marlene hadn't seen her children in nearly a year. Her daughter's high school graduation was her chance to reconnect and begin to rebuild their relationship. Feeling guilty for having left her daughter's father, and for having been absent for so long, she chickened out and didn't show up—yet again.

Closely intertwined with shame and regret, guilt shows up in many different ways in divorce and nearly every divorce has at least one party who is feeling some sort of guilt, shame or regret. Merriam-Webster Dictionary defines guilt as: 1) the fact of having committed a breach of conduct especially violating law and involving a penalty; 2) the state of one who has committed an offense especially consciously; feelings of culpability especially for imagined offenses or from a sense of inadequacy; self-reproach; 3) a feeling of culpability for offenses.

Guilt comes from a sense that you have done something wrong. The guilt may be from feeling that you have committed an offense against your spouse or children (that they won't grow up in a home with two parents, etc.) or your God (divorce often has religious ramifications). Guilt is regret that has been fed hormones and steroids and has grown out of control.

"I just want out."

Oftentimes, at least one of the three "Deadly Marriage Sins" are present—Abuse, Addiction and Adultery. If any one of the three, or a combination, is present, guilt flows freely. If either spouse committed any of one the "Deadly Marriage Sins," divorce is not only a consideration, but the judging public will expect it—and condone it.

What if none of the "Deadly Marriage Sins" is available as a reason to get a divorce? Your reasons are much less overt. Perhaps you honestly no longer love each other; you've grown apart. Perhaps you no longer have anything in common. You never fight and maybe you even consider the other person to be a good friend, but you no longer want to be married. Guilt will make its presence known in this situation because you will question whether you are making the right decision. You will wonder if you should stay in the marriage because things aren't dreadful.

Society has established the ideal that we get married and stay married until we are parted by death. This ideal was created thousands of years ago, when life expectancy hovered around 40 years of age. Today, living robustly into our 90s is common. Being able to choose a life mate that will be the absolute right one for potentially 70 years is an extremely tall task. People evolve, change and develop in different ways and at different paces. Sometimes, we get lucky and find that person who will progress in the same way we do. Sometimes, that person serves a purpose in our lives for a period of time, but the relationship has a natural life cycle that comes to an end organically when it begins to outlive its usefulness. It doesn't make one of you wrong and the other one right. It just is. Free from story and free from guilt. But that may not stop you from feeling guilty about it.

As if the guilt you feel naturally isn't bad enough, there are others who take fiendish delight, practically ensuring that you feel guilty. From your soon-to-be former spouse to your children, friends, co-workers and sometimes, even your own parents or family, everybody has an opinion (or more likely, judgment) about how you should conduct your life. They may do this by casting shadows of doubt on your decision. Because we spend an inordinate amount of time trying to look good and avoiding looking bad to others, this is precisely the type of interaction that has a deleterious effect on you.

Many times, I have had conversations with clients in which they are describing any number of scenarios where either they feel guilty about something or someone who is fanning the flames of guilt for them. What I tell them is what I am going to tell you here. Feeling guilty serves no purpose whatsoever. Becoming a masochist and crawling into a hole does not change the past or the present. It does not take away what you did or did not do. It does not heal the other person's hurt or anger. What it does do, however, is affect *your* future.

The impact of guilt on negotiations in a divorce is huge—and usually not positive for at least one of the parties. Guilt becomes the third entity in a negotiation and is definitely a foe. In the context of negotiation, usually the party who feels the most guilt will respond in one of two ways. The first way goes something like this: "I am horrible. I don't deserve to have anything. Please just don't hate me forever. Please don't tell all of our friends and family what a schmuck I am. Just take whatever you want. You deserve it and I should crawl into a cave." This person has become their own worst enemy, and without careful supervision, might give away the entire proverbial farm and all the animals on it. The second way that guilt shows up is more difficult to spot because it sends signals to attempt to throw you off the trail. This person throws his or her guilt onto the other person, usually in an angry, forceful and vengeful way. This charming party will highly litigate the case, taking unreasonable positions in order to attempt to extort the other person into giving them what they want. While this kind of behavior seems counterintuitive for a person who is feeling guilty, it makes perfect sense. The other party is attempting to create a lot of noise around the "guilty" person in order to deflect wrongdoing away from themselves.

Regardless of whether you are more like the first kind of guilty person or more like the second, one thing is clear: Guilt does not serve you, especially in negotiations. The end result is that the guilty party will end up with an unsatisfying result, one that will likely be filled with regret.

You are good a person who was created by the universe for a purpose. You may or may not have behaved badly. The first step to overcoming guilt is separating who you are from how you behaved. Parents can be angry at their child but still know that they are inherently good. Give yourself that same benefit of the doubt. You are not your behavior.

Do not mix your feelings of regret and culpability with the integrity of the legal process. Allow your divorce negotiations to be driven by law and equity—and not your feelings of guilt. Separating these will be your first step in relieving yourself of these poisonous feelings.

The next step is to look forward and not back. Philosopher Eckhart Tolle explains in *The Power of Now* that the past no longer exists. You can't go back and touch it, interact with it, or be with it. It is gone. The future doesn't exist either. The only moment that exists is the present moment. I recall a saying that has stuck with me: "Don't be stressed over something in your past, because there is nothing you can do to change it. Focus on your present and create your future."

Seize your present moment and decide that this moment for yourself will be free from guilt and regret.

Day 16 Exercise

Write out the following in your journal:

1. The major things you think you have done wrong, and the ones your spouse thinks you have done wrong. These things are not necessarily the same but it is important to write down both. Be honest. Write it all down.
2. Write the ways in which you might be able to change the things you have done wrong or your spouse thinks you have done wrong. (Yes, trick question.)
3. Write about the ways you have allowed your guilt to impact you and those around you.
4. Write down how you are going to seize your present moment today. What will that look like?

Day 16 Meditation/Affirmation

"The past is gone and the future is uncertain. Today, I am focusing on the present moment and will make it the best for me and for those around me."

Day 17

GRIEF

Renowned psychiatrist Elisabeth Kubler-Ross, in her 1969 book, *On Death and Dying*, forever changed how people perceive grief when she proffered her groundbreaking "Five Stages of Grief." In her work with dying patients, she found that both the dying person and their grieving loved ones work through stages of denial, anger, bargaining, depression and acceptance. These elements may not occur in a particular order, although acceptance is the final stage.

Divorce, while not exactly the same as the death of a spouse, shares several common experiences or emotions with the process of death. Both involve major transitions, loss, change and acquiring new skills. In both death and divorce, you end up without a spouse. In both scenarios, there is a grieving process and the stages are similar. Often, there is clearly anger. Denial and depression are frequently issues that arise. Bargaining, which I would say falls with my chapter on "Grasping" in this book, can be present. Finally, there will eventually be an acceptance that your life has forever changed.

Divorce and death are also very different. In death, there is no stigma; it is one of the few certainties in life. Thus, there is a dignity in death that divorce often lacks. In death, the spouse is gone completely. In divorce, the ex-spouse may still live in the same community, perhaps continuing to engage in distasteful, repugnant or disrespectful behaviors. In death, people surround you with love and support. During a divorce, friends and neighbors aren't generally showing up at your door with flowers and casseroles. In death, in most instances, the spouse inherits everything. In divorce, at best, the spouse receives half of the assets.

Grief is a necessary emotion in any transition. Feeling sorrow for what might have been, wistful about the good times, or sadness about the loss of your marriage is a normal part of the healing process. Each of us goes into a marriage believing that the relationship will last for the rest of our lifetime. It is natural to mourn for what might have been.

Allowing yourself the space to grieve and feel each of the emotions is healthy. During this time, the grief will manifest itself in a variety of ways. You might be feeling depressed or tired, or have trouble sleeping. Some deal with the stress by going back to smoking long after they have quit, or drinking more alcohol than usual. Some people gain weight; others lose weight. Some feel a generalized sense of increased tension, stress or sadness.

Depression during divorce is very common. Its roots can be in your story, your self-esteem, your anger, your despair, your loneliness. Whatever its cause, depression is very real and impacts your life in every way. Feeling that you cannot escape the acute pain you are experiencing leads to further feelings of despondency. I have always found this little vignette from *How the Grinch Stole Christmas* amusing because it light-heartedly illustrates a dark human condition: how truly low we can feel when we are suffering:

> **Grinch:** Nerve of those Whos. Inviting me down there on such short notice. Even if I wanted to go, my schedule wouldn't allow it! (flips his datebook open)
> 4:00: Wallow in self-pity

4:30: Stare into the abyss
5:00: Solve world hunger—tell no one
5:30: Jazzercise
6:30: Dinner with me—I can't cancel that again
7:00: Wrestle with my self-loathing….
I'm booked! Of course, if I bump the loathing to 9:00, I'll probably still have time to lie in my bed, stare at the ceiling and slip slowly into madness.

Seeking professional help often gives people some guidance and relief. Simply having another person with whom you can discuss issues, cry or vent is often therapeutic. Professionals also can prescribe anti-anxiety medications if necessary. This is especially important to do if you find that your grief is consuming you. If your anger or depression is dominating your life and you are having trouble functioning in your daily routine, don't hesitate to get professional help.

Divorce can be one of the most stressful events to endure. Some say it is the most stressful experience in their life. Thus, it is essential to move through the transition in the most optimum manner you can, and allow yourself the freedom to feel your grief in that process. Allow yourself the intimate time and space you need to cry.

What doesn't kill you really does make you stronger. Shifting your thoughts from negative to positive will help you begin to feel better. Whenever you have a negative thought, replace it with a positive one. Buddha said, "Your thoughts create your reality. What you think, you become." Start by naming 10 things a day for which you are grateful. Once the majority of your thoughts become positive, instead of mostly negative, you will enter into the acceptance stage, and your life will truly change.

Day 17 Exercise

Write in your journal:

Today I am sad about_____.

I grieve for_____.

The reason I grieve for this is_____.

The way this grief is showing up in my life is _____
_____.

(For instance: I am angry. I am smoking again. I have gained weight. I haven't been sleeping.)

Ten things I am grateful for are:_____.

Now look at this list of things for which you are grateful at least 10 times today. Decide you will name 10 things for which you are grateful every morning.

Day 17 Meditation/Affirmation

"I will allow myself the time I need to feel my grief. Then I will focus on what I am grateful for and focus on my positive thoughts."

Day 18

APATHY

For many years in my first marriage, I tried and tried to make it work. I suggested counseling, date nights and dinners at home alone after putting the children to bed. I tried asking nicely, and also stooped low by attempting to manipulate and guilt him into being interested in the marriage. The response was always similar, and sounded something like this: "I am not talking to a shrink. I am too tired. We don't have the money to go out. I am not a talker and you know that." I finally gave up.

For several years, neither of us put an ounce of effort into fanning the flames of romance. We had three small children, and both worked full time, so finding other diversions was not hard. There were soccer games to coach and dance recitals to attend; pinewood derby cars to build for Boy Scouts and cookies to sell for Girl Scouts. There were bills to pay, a house to maintain, and homework to do. This scene from Nora Ephron's movie, *Heartburn*, starring Meryl Streep, sums it up:

> It is possible to...to love someone so much, or to think that you want to love them so much that you just don't even see anything. You decide to love him. And you decide to trust him, and you're in the marriage. And you're in the day-to-

dayness of the marriage and...you sort of notice that things are not the way they were, but it's...it's a...a distant bell. And then when things do turn out to have been wrong, it's not that you knew all along. It's just that you were...somewhere else.

Eventually, I woke up and realized that ours was no longer a marriage. My revelation arrived during a typical Little League baseball game. One of the mothers showed up breathless and eager to share the news that she and her husband were going to spend an entire weekend away alone—without the kids. She was brimming with excitement. I distinctly remember having an "aha moment" when my first reaction to her news was that I had no desire to be alone with my husband for an hour—let alone a whole weekend.

By the time I realized what was going on in *my* marriage, I no longer wanted to be in my marriage. As much as my first husband was a good father and a good man, I felt complete apathy about the marriage. In fact, the last year we were married, my birthday went by and he didn't acknowledge it—not even with a Hallmark card. Neither of us really even noticed. There was no conversation we had with each other that couldn't have been broadcast on a PA system throughout the neighborhood. Our communication had distilled down to: "I'll pick up the boys from soccer," followed by, "Okay. I'll stop at the grocery store on the way home."

When we decided to divorce, people were surprised because we never fought. But we had become indifferent toward the marriage. I finally made the decision that if I was going to be alone, I wanted to be genuinely alone. That would at least give me the opportunity to find the right person.

Apathy is a warning sign in your marriage. It can be caused by depression or the feeling of a lack of control. In my case, it was a reaction to feeling helpless. Apathy is not an empowered state. It is a reactive state. It can stem from a day-to-day chipping away at the relationship: each time your spouse doesn't remember your birthday, or doesn't tackle tasks and projects they agreed to do around the house or with the children. Not keeping small agreements quietly erodes the relationship. Over time, small erosions can be just as toxic as one of the "Three Deadly Marriage Sins" (abuse, addiction and adultery). Eventually, after years of unfulfilled expectations, you react by no longer caring or being engaged in the relationship.

When you become aware of your lack of emotion in a relationship, you begin the process of taking back your life. Being apathetic does not coexist with growth or motivation. Conquering apathy begins with taking action. Figuring out what you want, the steps to get there and how you are going to implement them will get you out of the apathy slump. Overcoming inertia is the biggest hurdle. With each step you take, you will feel more and more motivated to create your new life.

Day 18 Exercise

1. Write down what you want for your life. If it is to stay married, then what does that marriage look like? If it is to be divorced, then what does that look like?
2. Write down the steps you are going to take to make what you want a reality.
3. Make a daily calendar and schedule when you will be taking the steps.
4. Check off each step when you have completed it.

Day 18 Meditation/Affirmation

"I care enough about myself to set goals and take action to make sure I reach them."

Day 19

RESIGNATION

How do you know it is time to leave? Clearly, if one of the "Three Deadly Marriage Sins" (abuse, addiction and adultery) is present, ending the marriage has probably crossed your mind. It might also be an option you're considering if you are unhappy, you've grown apart, or you're constantly bickering.

Relationships are like live plants. To flourish, they need to be fed and nurtured. For a long time, the plants continue to grow and thrive. Then sometimes, even if you have given them tender care, they begin to show signs of struggle, as if they are dying. After trying a new type of fertilizer, they begin to flourish again and thrive for many more years. Sometimes, however, the plants stop blossoming and the leaves fall off. No amount of care and attention can save them.

In marriages, we also have to nurture and feed the relationship and each other in order for it to grow and thrive. Sometimes, when it becomes struggle and effort, by nourishing it with date nights, attention to each other, attending marriage classes and counseling, it will perk up and bloom again. At other times, even though you are trying harder and harder to save it, it just cannot be revived. Here is a list of some signs that your marriage may be over:

1. There is abuse (physical, mental or emotional) in the marriage that continues and is impacting your life negatively.
2. There is addiction in the marriage that continues and is impacting your life negatively.
3. There is adultery in the marriage by one or both parties which has irreparably undermined either one's trust.
4. There is no physical relationship or if there is, you aren't interested in it. (A friend confided in me that toward the end of her marriage, she would try to position herself during sex so that she could watch television.)
5. You are constantly at odds with one another, and have begun fighting in public.
6. You have started fantasizing about what it would be like not to be married anymore.
7. You find yourself compromising morals, values and beliefs that are important to you.
8. You feel that you can't be yourself in the relationship.
9. You no longer care about working on the marriage and have no interest in being alone with your spouse.
10. You find that, despite your best efforts, the unhappy times have begun to outnumber the good times.

By realizing that sometimes relationships were just not meant to last forever, you can give up on coming up with reasons to make the other person wrong. The marriage just did not last; and that's okay. Leaving behind your anger, guilt and despair will create an opening of space for you, a clearing. At that time, you can take a look at the other person and decide whether this person can be part of a healthy future for you. Make sure you are seeing the person in every way that they are and every way that they are not—not who you think they *are going* to be. Or consider this question: Is this person now a part of my past?

A period of separation can be beneficial when the time apart is used to work on the marriage. Living in separate quarters often provides some insight into whether this is what you actually want. Some states require a specified separation prior to the filing of divorce and other states do not.

Resignation to the idea of divorce happens at different stages for each person. For some, it is before the divorce is filed; for others it occurs during the divorce process. Sadly, for some, it takes place long after the divorce has been final. Coming to terms with the situation depends on who initiated the divorce discussions in the first place. Being resigned to it (approaching it with an unresisting attitude—an acquiescence) does not mean you are happy about it or that you want it.

Day 19 Exercise

Look at the list and determine which, if any apply, to your marriage. If they do, then determine whether it is time for you be ready to resign yourself to the idea that continuing the marriage is the best decision for you or your spouse. You each deserve the opportunity to live your best life.

Day 19 Meditation/Affirmation

"I accept the things I cannot change; I have the courage to change the things I can; and I have the wisdom to know the difference."

Day 20

DIGNITY

D*ivorce with dignity. Is this an oxymoron?* Some think so. Once you have made the decision to divorce, simultaneously decide that it will be a divorce with dignity. What is a divorce with dignity? Does it mean one in which you roll over and give your ex-spouse everything? Does it mean being demure or non-assertive in the process? Strictly playing nice? Not necessarily.

Threading your way through the process of divorce is humbling for even the strongest among us. Dignity allows you to wend your way through the darkness while making fewer wrong turns. It serves as a beacon of light when your footing becomes unsteady.

As I discussed in "Day 6: Blame," the Latin root "dign" of the word dignity means "worth." You are worthy, and so are your children and your ex-husband, of a rational and equitable process for the dissolution of your marriage.

Divorcing with dignity is not tearing each other to shreds, leaving each other bloodied and bruised in the process. It is not sharing intimate details about your personal lives with others. It is not using your children to exact revenge against your spouse. It is not litigating every possible issue. Dignity is not vengeful, nor is it ruthless and unforgiving. As we have established, those types of emotions do not serve you and in the long run, and they are far more toxic to you than to anyone else. You cannot be filled with negativity and expect positivity to appear. Dignity doesn't make the other person wrong and blame them for the demise of the marriage.

Dignity does mean ensuring that the principles of justice and equity are served. If you are entitled to half the assets, then pursue it. If you are entitled to support, then certainly expect to receive it. If you believe your spouse is asking for more than what is equitable then proceed to court. Dignity means respecting yourself as well as your spouse.

Divorce with dignity is free from intimidation. Recently, I met with Diana, who cheated on her husband. Upon his discovery of the affair, her husband set off on a frenzied rampage texting the boyfriend, boyfriend's wife, Diana's parents and her family members. He threatened to go to her boss and "take her down." Physically shaking with worry and fear, she tearfully shared that she didn't know what to do. I told her to own her mistakes. Go to her boss, her friends—to anyone who mattered to her—and tell them what happened. Then I instructed her to go to the marital home, with friends, and speak to him about dividing the furniture. I warned her not to let him bully her and that if he threatened her, to go to the police and get a restraining order. As we spoke, she became visibly stronger and her tears began to dry.

That evening, she went back to the home with a friend, and calmly and respectfully told him that she wouldn't be daunted by his threats. Remarkably, he backed off. He apologized and admitted that he was so hurt that he wanted her to feel how hurt he was. By approaching him with respect, he responded in kind. Had she entered the home blazing with anger, he most assuredly would not have reacted calmly.

A divorce with dignity is one in which both parties feel respected and valued throughout the process. This choice takes courage and integrity. By choosing to be courageous, you leave no room for fear. By choosing integrity, you create the space for joy. True rewards will come from approaching the process with respect, honor, integrity and dignity.

Day 20 Exercise

1. Journal what your divorce with dignity will look like for you. Create a list of 10 things that a divorce with dignity is. Decide this will be your "Ten Commandments" during the divorce (commandments which you will not violate).
2. Create a list of 10 things that a divorce with dignity is not. Decide these will be your deadly sins during the divorce and you will not engage in these behaviors.

Day 20 Meditation/Affirmation

"My divorce will be a divorce with dignity. I have the courage to respect myself and my spouse throughout the process."

Section Two

Physical FREEDOM

Day 21

KNOWLEDGE

The shock is wearing off. You have decided to move ahead with the divorce. Your head must stay in the game while you're grappling with strong emotions and your heart is working overtime. The great paradox in a divorce is that while you're overwhelmed with the flood of emotions dealing with one of the most difficult transitions you'll ever experience, you also have to be sure that you are thinking more clearly than ever because your choices and actions during this time will impact the rest of your life. No problem at all, right?

Imagine you are going on a hike deep in forested mountains. You have to make sure that you pack the right provisions and essential equipment in order to survive. The process of divorce will often feel like one of survival. It is time to pack your survival kit—your bag of knowledge. Like a wilderness expedition, the more you are prepared, the easier the journey.

What will you need in your kit?

1. <u>Take stock of every asset and every liability you have.</u> Get intimately acquainted with your financial picture. Find out how your assets are titled. This includes your bank accounts, your real estate,

your automobiles, everything. Find out what assets are in your spouse's name, including gifts or inheritances. Right now, your job is to be a sleuth to gain as much information as you possibly can. Find out about your debt load as individuals and as a couple. Get a copy of your credit report and make sure that it is in harmony with what you believe your liabilities should be. Examine your real estate holdings as individuals and as a couple to determine whose name they are in, and what the mortgage balances are. Make copies of every statement or shred of financial information you can find. This includes all statements for: bank, credit card, retirement accounts, brokerage accounts, mortgage(s) and other loans. Hunt down big-ticket receipts and other financial information that may be critical. If you can't make copies, take pictures with your smartphone.

2. <u>Open your own bank and credit card accounts.</u> This applies especially if you are the non-monied spouse. Your attorney may be able to get you some temporary support down the road, but it may take a few months. Be sure you have a way to support yourself for a period of time. If you don't have credit in your own name, applying for a credit card is an easy way to establish a line of credit.

3. <u>Determine what your spouse's income is.</u> Find a recent Social Security statement, income tax returns, W-2s, K-1s, or 1099s. Sometimes this area can be a little tricky. If your spouse owns a business and the business pays personal expenses, those expenses may be characterized as spousal income in the divorce case. Locate financial documents on the business, such as tax returns, general ledgers and income, and bank and QuickBooks statements. Again, make copies of everything you find.

4. <u>Determine your true living expenses.</u> This includes all expenses: monthly mortgage or rent, utilities, automobile (including insurance, fuel and maintenance), groceries, children's needs, entertainment, beauty and hygiene and pet care. Every dollar you spend will count in a divorce.

5. <u>Create a post-divorce budget.</u> Include all of the living expenses just as you did for your current expenses, but now project what your expenses will be after the divorce.

6. <u>Determine what your current estate plan provides.</u> If you have had a formal estate plan completed, obtain copies. If it has been a while since you have had it created, review it to determine to whom you've designated as your: power of attorney, health-care surrogate, trustees, executor and beneficiaries. You may want to change those prior to the case being filed. Some courts issue orders when divorce cases are filed which preclude changes during the pendency of the action.

7. <u>Determine the beneficiaries of your retirement accounts.</u> Confirm who you've designated. Again, you may want to change these prior to filing your action for divorce.

8. <u>Determine what you want to do about your living situation.</u> If you jointly own the home, and you want to sell the home or let your spouse remain there after the divorce, then vacating the home may be fine. On the other hand, if you want to keep the home to live in during and after the divorce, or the home is in your spouse's name, then do not move out. Moving out can impact your chances of receiving exclusive occupancy of the home during the pendency of

the divorce. Note: In domestic violence situations, this may change the way the court perceives the move, so discuss the options with your attorney.

9. <u>Change your passwords.</u> Change passwords to all of your accounts: financial, email, social media like Facebook and all others.

10. <u>Line up your support team.</u> Find a good therapist with whom you feel comfortable or speak to your church pastor. Make sure you have a few friends or family members around who are ready to listen.

Day 21 Exercise

Go through Items 1-10. Start making a list of where you can get the information or to whom you should speak to get the information. Decide that you will do one item on the list each day until it is completed.

Day 21 Meditation/Affirmation

"I am building the proper tool kit to ensure that this life transition is as smooth as possible for my family and me."

Day 22

ATTORNEYS

The time has come.

One of the first questions that can arise is: Should you hire an attorney or should you try to make the journey alone? The answer is always to hire a lawyer if you can. Even the simplest of divorces are not always as simple as you might think. The worst initial consultations I have are the ones in which someone who managed their own divorce to save money is now seeking to mop up the mess. Documents are typically inadequate. Once the final judgment has been entered, it cannot be undone and at best is very difficult to modify. Don't be penny-wise and pound-foolish.

Finding the right attorney can be daunting. If you have no idea where to begin, start by asking another attorney you might know in the community. Local Bar associations tend to be smaller and more closely knit, and the attorneys usually know each other. If you don't know an attorney, ask a trusted friend or other professionals for references. If those avenues don't prove fruitful; Internet research also is useful.

Choose at least two names and interview each one in person. Don't be offended if the attorney won't speak to you on the telephone prior to the meeting. Often an exploratory assessment needs to be performed to ensure that there is no conflict of interest. For example, it needs to be confirmed that your spouse has not met with the attorney first because that would preclude you from using the firm's services. Be aware that divorce attorneys often charge a fee for initial consultations. This is used as a disincentive for one of the spouses to interview all of the local divorce attorneys to intentionally create a conflict, which would strip the other spouse's ability to hire a good attorney.

Once your appointment is made, compile all of your financial information and documentation to take with you to the consultation. The more specific you can be, the more specific the attorney can be in assessing your case. Ask how much of the attorney's practice is devoted to family law matters, and how long the attorney has been practicing law. Most importantly, go with your intuition. Do you feel comfortable with this person, who will be the captain of your journey to becoming single again? You want to be certain that you have confidence in your legal captain's navigation skills.

Attorneys cannot represent both parties, so if you and your spouse want to work with only one professional, you might want to consider hiring a neutral mediator. The caveat to this approach is that the mediator is then not representing either of you and is simply working to establish an agreeable resolution.

Divorce lawyers either charge by the hour (these are the better ones) or charge a flat rate for a particular task. It is not ethical for marital and family lawyers to have a contingency arrangement (meaning that they only get paid if you get paid) with their fee tied to the outcome of the case. You will execute a retainer agreement and most likely pay the attorney a refundable retainer and the services you receive will be billed against it. Some attorneys elect to have a portion of the retainer be nonrefundable, so read your retainer agreement carefully. At the end of each month, you should receive a detailed bill, which also will give you an update on how much of your retainer is left. Once the retainer monies have been exhausted, you will be asked to replenish until the case is resolved. The retainer agreement also should outline the procedures should you have a dispute with the bill. Usually, you have a period of time to contest, and if you fail to bring forth your issues within that timeframe, the bill is considered correct.

Expect to be billed for everything that requires the lawyer's time or the paralegal's time on your case. Being charged for costs such as copies, postage, court filing fees and court reporters is standard as well. High-end attorneys may charge an "engagement fee" which is considered "earned when paid." This means that if you decide to stop working with that attorney, you will not get that portion back.

Finally, make sure you tell your lawyer everything. Your relationship with your lawyer must be based on honesty and integrity. You won't get your best possible representation if your lawyer doesn't have all the facts. So, tell all—hairy warts included. Lawyers who practice in this field have heard it all. And I mean "IT ALL." There is almost nothing you can say that would be too shocking or earth-shattering. We hear stories of crazy sex lives, weird addictions, strange relationship interactions and unethical business practices. Everything. Believe me, whatever you don't tell, will definitely come out on the other side, usually at an inopportune moment, like say, *in front of the judge*. So don't hold back. The more honest you can be, the better your lawyer will be equipped to advocate for you and your position, and defend you.

Day 22 Exercise

Get at least two or three names of attorneys and make appointments with them. Make a list of questions that you have for them and make sure to take along the financial information you have gathered.

Day 22 Meditation/Affirmation

"I look forward to meeting with my attorney because I know it is an important step toward my freedom and my newly created positive life."

Day 23

LAW

What's the difference between divorce "law" and divorce "justice"? People behave badly at times. Usually, leading up to a divorce, at least one party has behaved badly. At least, that's the story the other party is telling. During a divorce, both parties usually take a few turns engaging in conduct that might be slightly unbecoming. "Criminal attorneys see bad people at their best and divorce attorneys see good people at their worst" is a common saying in the legal world. There is a certain level of irrationality that creeps in during a divorce, and it often doesn't dissipate for a couple of years. Once the transition is complete and separate lives are being led, common sense reappears and the madness slowly dissipates. Until then, it can be Thunderdome!

So what's the difference between divorce law and divorce justice? Divorce "laws" differ by state but the basic elements are similar. Typically, there are laws guiding property settlement, support or alimony, parenting plans (custody arrangements) and child support. Divorce courts have to be equitable (meaning equally fair and reasonable). Judges basically take a day or two to hear each person's version of the story, then they make a ruling that you have to live with. You can appeal the decision if you think the judge made a legal error, e.g., radically deviated from your state's laws. The law is the law, and you can't change it. Your lawyer can attempt to argue your position in light of the law and argue that the law be applied in a particular manner, but for the most part, the law will guide the judge's decisions.

Divorce "justice" is what clients *want* to happen. In the film *A Christmas Story*, Ralphie fantasizes that his teacher will be swept off her feet by his essay and give it an A+. Likewise, clients routinely believe that the judge will see what a maniacal, lying, unsupportive sack of crapola their soon-to-be ex-spouse is and they will get everything awarded to them. Some imagine that the judge will give the Ex a humiliating smack-down that will forever shame and sting.

In reality, conversations like this occur all the time:

WIFE: He is so horrible for insinuating that I should have to go back to work after I was a devoted wife to him and mother to his children for all of these years. He still makes $500,000 a year and has a new girlfriend. He won't let the kids call me when they are with him. His new girlfriend is a gold digger. She told the kids that I am a "whacko" and he agreed with her. He went on a trip with her and didn't even invite the kids. Won't the judge see how horrible he is? We need to file a motion immediately to get him and his new girlfriend to stop disparaging me.

ATTORNEY: Yes, the judge will see how horrible he is. The judge also will hear about your new boyfriend and the unflattering characterizations you have shared with the children—that your husband was abusive and controlling, and he doesn't care about anyone but himself.

Remember: The judges who are sitting on the divorce bench listen to bickering couples *all day, every day*. No matter how horrible you think your spouse has been, if you live in a no-fault state, the judge will apply the law and move on to the next case.

Courts are not fairy tales and judges are not fairy godmothers. Their gavels are not magic wands that can be waved, suddenly forcing your Ex to grow a conscience, be supportive or fair, or act responsibly. They also cannot spin straw into gold. The amount of assets (and debt) that you have along with the amount of income you both make is a black-and-white fact. Often, for one reason or another, people think they are entitled to more. Courts simply won't give you most or all of your former spouse's assets or income simply because you feel entitled to it.

Choose your battles carefully. You want to be the one wearing the white hat. Behave yourself to the letter during the divorce. Everything you do and say may end up being repeated in court. You don't want to appear like fighting children ("He started it!"…."Nah-ah, she did!") because the judge will simply conclude you are two people who can't get along. Only go to court when it is truly warranted.

Listen to your lawyer. Heed the advice when you're told that your expectations are exceeding the reality of the law and reevaluate your demands. Court is not the place for dichotomous concepts such as: winner and loser; deserving and undeserving; righteous and corrupt; or angels and demons. The reality is that if you go to court, you don't get justice, you get a decision. To get there, you spend lots and lots of money and tear each other apart along the way. People don't usually come out of trial better friends. There are no winners in divorce court, except maybe the divorce lawyers.

Day 23 Exercise

You'll need two sheets of paper. Meet with your lawyer or do some research. Find out what the laws are and how they apply to your situation. Figure out what your best-case scenario is and what your worst-case scenario is. Write them down on one sheet of paper. On the second sheet of paper, write down what you think the outcome *should* be if "justice" is served. Compare your desired outcome to your worst-case scenario. How far apart are the two? Worlds away? Or fairly close? If they are worlds away, give up on justice and punishment and declare your new future by writing out what that will be.

Day 23 Meditation/Affirmation

"Today, I will focus on what the law provides for me in this divorce—nothing more and nothing less."

Day 24

PROPERTY

"This is my stuff, that's your stuff, that'll be his stuff over there. That's all you need in life, a little place for your stuff. That's all your house is: a place to keep your stuff. If you didn't have so much stuff, you wouldn't need a house. You could just walk around all the time."
— *George Carlin*

Comedian George Carlin was a brilliant observer of interactions and the human condition who could spin the rote details of life into a humorous and insightful monologue. His "Stuff" routine is especially interesting when considered in light of marriage. During the course of a marriage, you and your spouse accumulate stuff. You also earn stuff during the marriage, such as money, retirement benefits or stock options. Sometimes you bring stuff into the marriage. Other times, people give you stuff while you're married. At the end of the marriage, bestowed upon the judge is the honor of dividing up all that stuff. How does that happen?

THREE PILES

First, the court will create three piles: his, hers, theirs. The "theirs" pile is the one that gets divided between each party. What goes into the "his" pile or the "hers" pile? Anything you or your spouse brought into the marriage, such as what you owned prior to the marriage (there are exceptions to this) or what was given to you as a gift from a third party during the marriage. Separate property can include retirement accounts that were funded prior the marriage, investment accounts you had prior to the marriage, an inheritance received prior to or during the marriage *that has been kept separate*, and real estate you owned prior to the marriage.

Alert! Do not commingle (mix) your income or earnings with any asset that you want to keep separate. (Income and earnings are generally marital unless you signed a prenuptial agreement which says that they are not.) Don't mix separate assets in joint accounts or with other joint assets. This includes retirement funds, bank accounts, investments and real estate—anything. For example, I've had clients who used their inheritance to purchase real estate or to put in a joint account for purposes of creating collateral for a loan. Then funds were returned back into the separate account. If you can provide the paper trail, a court *might* accept it if you have excellent records, but it *might not*. It also just might declare that the assets have been commingled. Too bad, so sad: The assets are now considered joint.

No-fault states are governed by the doctrine of "equitable distribution." You don't have to prove any reason why you want a divorce other than that the marriage is irretrievably broken. Remember that "equitable" is not necessarily synonymous with "equal." Technically, equitable means fair or based upon the principles of equity, which often means an equal division, but there are times when a court can decide that in order to achieve an equitable result, an unequal division of the marital pot of assets is warranted. Some states still require that the spouse who is requesting a divorce prove grounds or fault on the other party, such as abuse, adultery or other reasons. In these states, the court can split the marital assets unequally as a punitive measure based upon the grounds for dissolution.

ASSET AND LIABILITY SUMMARY

To keep track of the assets and liabilities, and for ease of division, your lawyer will create a spreadsheet which will include everything in the three piles. If there is a liability against a certain asset, it will be reflected. The asset or debt will be placed into the column of the spouse who is keeping it. If the asset is a piece of real estate that might be sold, then the net value (after closing costs, transfer fees, etc.) will be reflected. If the asset is a retirement account for which no income taxes have been paid, then the income tax will be reflected in order to achieve the true net value. The spreadsheet will look similar to this:

#	Description	Fair Market Value	Liabilities	Transfer/ Tax Effect	Net Value	Husband – Marital	Wife – Marital	Husband – Nonmarital	Wife – Nonmarital
1	123 Oak Ave. Anytown, USA	$300,000	($100,000)	($21,000)	$179,000	$89,500	$89,500		
2	Bank account #4558	$20,000			$20,000	$10,000	$10,000		
3	Bank account #1221 (Wife's inheritance)	$50,000			$50,000				$50,000
4	Wife's IRA	$75,000		($15,000)	$60,000	$30,000	$30,000		
5	Husband's gift from parents in bank account #2222	$30,000			$30,000			$30,000	
6	Joint savings account #3333	$100,000			$100,000	$50,000	$50,000		
7	Boat	$25,000	($5,000)		$20,000	$20,000			
8	Car 2012 Toyota	$30,000	($15,000)		$15,000		$15,000		
9	Car 2010 Truck	$40,000			$40,000	$40,000			
10	Credit card #4444		($5,000)		($5,000)	($2,500)	($2,500)		
	SUBTOTALS	$670,000	($125,000)		$509,000	$237,000	$192,000	$30,000	$50,000
	DIFFERENTIAL					$45,000	$45,000		
	EQUALIZER PAYMENT					($22,500)	$22,500		
	TOTALS					$214,500	$214,500		

In our fictional scenario above, the parties are selling the marital home. Once it sells, the parties will split the net proceeds. The husband's car has more equity in it than the wife's car, and he is keeping the boat. As a result, he has more of the marital asset pile than she does. Therefore, he will have to pay the equalizer payment of $22,500. The equalizer payment is just what it sounds like: a payment made from one spouse to the other to "equalize" the marital assets. He can do this in a variety of different ways. She could get the $22,500 from his share of the net proceeds of the home, he could give her more from his share of the joint savings account, or any other way they decide works best for them. Notice that his assets and her assets are carved from the "theirs" pile.

After the spreadsheet is created, the math is easy. The trick with these things can be what value goes onto the spreadsheet. Parties squabble all the time about what the value of the house, cars or jewelry should be. Appraisals can help, but sometimes even those values are challenged if they aren't to an individual's liking. Appraisals can be done on just about anything, including jewelry, artwork and furniture. If one party owns a business that was created during the marriage, that is a marital asset. Valuing a business and figuring out how to split it equitably can be a big challenge. In these cases, a forensic accountant may be helpful. It's true that it will drive up the cost of the case, but it may be necessary.

The challenges of settling on a final spreadsheet are too numerous to list, but here are a couple of issues that can arise. Your spouse owns a house that was purchased prior the marriage but during the marriage, you paid the mortgage payments with your earnings. To the extent the mortgage principal was paid down during the marriage, that portion can be carved off and equitably distributed. Maybe you owned a house prior the marriage, but your spouse built an addition to it. Now your spouse claims that the property is worth more because of the addition. If that's the case, then the task is to figure how much value it gained and equitably distribute that piece of it.

Personal property is usually divided between the parties themselves, but can sometimes be placed on the spreadsheet or divided by a list that is attached to the final judgment or final agreement. Engagement rings are a non-marital gift to the wife that she gets to keep. (If a marriage doesn't take place, then he can rightfully get it back.)

SPLITTING RETIREMENT BENEFITS

If your head isn't already swimming, retirement benefits may have to be split by a special type of order called a Qualified Domestic Relations Order (QDRO). This is mechanism was created by the Internal Revenue Service specifically for divorcing couples. It allows one spouse to roll his or her share of the assets into another qualified account without creating a tax event. Usually, if you take money out of your 401(k) if you haven't reached mandatory age requirements, you will pay penalties. And no matter your age, you will pay income taxes on that withdrawal because the funds have not yet been taxed. A QDRO allows you to take your half of the money and put it into another retirement account without having to pay taxes or penalties.

PROPERTY SETTLEMENT FIRST

Generally, the property settlement portion of the case is completed first because it can impact the rest of the case. For example, if a spouse who is claiming a need for alimony receives an investment account that pays income, then that income will reduce the spouse's need for alimony. Child support also is based upon the incomes of both parties, so the property settlement will affect that calculation as well. Once this part is completed, then the parties can move to the next portion of the case. You are also one step closer to being free!

Day 24 Exercise

Based on the sample worksheet provided, begin creating your own spreadsheet. Start gathering critical values and enter them into the spreadsheet. Start thinking about which assets you might want to retain and which ones you think your spouse might want to retain. Place those into the respective columns. Continue to work through the spreadsheet throughout the process.

Day 24 Meditation/Affirmation

"I know that principles of equity will guide the division of assets and liabilities. I look forward to the feeling of relief when it is completed."

Day 25

ALIMONY

Alimony, spousal maintenance or spousal support—whatever term is used—is one of the most hotly-contested and litigated areas in all of marital law. This is a form of support or payments made by one spouse to the other spouse during or following the divorce to provide financial assistance.

Contrary to popular belief, alimony comes in more ways than one. Support can be ordered for a period of time for a specific purpose, or until one of you dies or the payee gets remarried. Support can be ordered during the pendency of the divorce case or until one party completes their education and for other reasons—but it's for a fixed period of time.

Alimony is tied to many different factors, including: the length of the marriage; whether one party needs it; whether the other party has the ability to pay it; and the disparity in incomes. The list goes on. Some states have guidelines to help the courts determine the award. In most cases, the courts have wide discretion to determine this issue.

Why is this so inflammatory? One reason goes back to what we discussed on Day 23. One party feels deserving but the other party doesn't agree. One party doesn't think it is "fair" that he or she has to share the hard-earned fruits of their labor after the marriage is dissolved. Sometimes it is a tool one spouse might want to employ to inflict pain upon the other spouse as payment for causing hurt. In other cases, one party has grown accustomed to a certain lifestyle and has no plans to change it despite the transition taking place.

I have had cases in which the wife wanted more than 50 percent of the husband's income and cases where the husband has willingly agreed to assuage his guilty conscience. (Then, of course, he regretted it almost immediately.) I also have been involved in cases where the husband wanted to pay the wife absolutely nothing after a long-term marriage during which he cheated. In these situations, he simply sees his income as his money, not hers. Period. In these circumstances, the judge will decide by: looking at her expenses and his ability to pay them; the couple's lifestyle during the marriage; the duration of the marriage; the health of both parties; whether they had an agreement that the wife would stay home to care for the children; and many other factors.

Alimony is generally taxable to the party who is receiving it (the payee) but the payer receives a tax deduction. You need to take this into account when determining alimony with your lawyer. If you need $5,000 a month, that amount needs to be adjusted higher to a pre-tax number so that you net $5,000. Typically, alimony is only modifiable when there has been a substantial change in circumstances; don't act under the false belief that you can make a deal and request a change the following year. If you try to modify an alimony amount, be prepared to prove a major life change, such as a disability, loss of a job (and that you've diligently tried to find another one) or that the payee spouse has remarried.

In any divorce, you will be required to submit a financial outline detailing your income and expenses, and your assets and liabilities. This will likely become a sworn document called an affidavit, which means you are swearing under oath to the court that the information is true. This financial outline will be used as the basis for determining one party's need for support and the other party's ability to pay it. That is why it is absolutely critical to think carefully about how much you actually spend monthly and annually on housing, automobile, groceries, grooming, vacations, pet, and children. Everything. Also carefully include all sources of revenue you receive. Make sure you are accurate, because if you deflate or inflate numbers, it will come out in court, and the other side will use that as an opportunity to impeach your credibility.

If you aren't sure what your current living expenses are, you might have to go back through your bank and credit card statements for the past year or two and piece a sound budget together. The categories you want to make sure you include are: housing (rent or mortgage, taxes, insurance, maintenance fees and repairs); automobiles (payments, gas, insurance, repairs and maintenance); food (groceries and dining out); household expenses (utilities, phone, pool, lawn and miscellaneous); personal (grooming, manicures, dry cleaning, medical, gifts); children's expenses (tuition, extracurricular activities, medical); and debts (loans, credit cards, etc.).

In addition to the financial outline you prepare for the court, which details your current expenses, create a separate one for your use that details your expected expenses. If you are planning to move to an apartment, indicate the new rent amount. You might have to do some research to determine what figures to use. This will help you determine a realistic budget. Share this with your lawyer so your future needs will be properly advocated for as you go forward.

Day 25 Exercise

Create two budgets. The first one calculates current expenses based on your lifestyle during the marriage. The second one will include your projected living expenses for your new life.

Day 25 Meditation/Affirmation

"I am enjoying the process of creating a budget for my new life because I can envision myself empowered and living free."

Day 26

PARENTING PLAN

Traditionally called custody or visitation, one of the most common terms today for describing when and with whom children will spend time following a divorce is parenting plan. Even more provocative than alimony, this can be one of the most heart-wrenching arenas of a divorce. Here are a few pointers to make this part go a little more smoothly for everyone involved:

BE RESPECTFUL!

Start by deciding right now that you will be respectful of the fact that your soon-to-be ex-spouse won't be your children's ex. A parent is a parent forever. Also remember that your children are half that person, so when you insult the other parent, you are insulting them. You might not see it that way, but children do. By fostering an environment of discord, you could be damaging your children emotionally and psychosocially—for life. It is not worth it. Keep your opinions to yourself, no matter how hard it is.

Allow your children some reasonable privacy in their relationship with the other parent. Forcing your children to become a spy in the other household and pressing them for information makes children uncomfortable. If your children want to call the other spouse while they are with you, allow them to do so within reason.

BE SPECIFIC!

When you create a plan, be as specific as you can. For example, the father will have the children from Mondays at 3 p.m. to Wednesday mornings, when he takes the children to school. The mother will have the children from Wednesday after school to Friday mornings, when she takes them to school. Each parent shall have every other weekend, which shall be defined as Fridays after school through Monday mornings, when that parent shall take them to school. If the children do not have school, the drop-off time will be 9 a.m. at the home of the parent who will be receiving the children.

In addition, account for each and every holiday, vacations, school breaks, Mother's Day, Father's Day, children's birthdays and parents' birthdays. Be specific with the times for each of these (for example 9 a.m. to 8 p.m.) as well as who is transporting the children.

Even if you think the arrangement is ideally set and you want to keep the schedule flexible and open, please include a plan in your agreement. New spouses and new lives cause unforeseen changes. If you have a backup plan upon which you can rely when things go awry, you will save yourself a lot of headaches and potential attorneys' fees down the road.

You also want to include who will be making medical and educational decisions for the children, and agree that both parents have access to this information.

If one parent wants to relocate, then include details about how the travel expenses will be handled, and craft a very specific plan. Ensure that your agreement dictates the consent of the parent who is not moving and the reasons for the move. If you don't want the other person to move out of the area without your written consent, make sure that is detailed in the agreement.

BEWARE!

If you cannot agree on these things, a court will make decisions for you. The court will examine every square inch of your life and your children's lives. You could have to parade into court every coach, teacher, grandparent, neighbor or friend in your kids' world. It isn't very fun and it is very expensive. The court will weigh many different factors to determine what plan is in the child's best interests. Chances are that you will get a decision neither of you like because —no matter how much information you cram into your trial—the judge cannot possibly know everything about your lives.

In truth, I have never seen a couple come out on the other side of trial better friends. Trials are antagonistic by nature. In order to get what you want, you will have to say all sorts of nasty things about the other parent. What are you really fighting for? If your spouse wants 15 overnights in a month, but you think there should only be 10, carefully consider how much those extra overnights are really worth in terms of time, money and emotional drain on the family.

BE FLEXIBLE!

Remember: You once thought enough of your former spouse to create children together. How you handle this situation can make or break life for your children. Friday afternoons can be a nightmare for divorce lawyers. That is when a lot of visitation exchanges take place. One time, a client called me on a Friday afternoon, and he was irate because his former wife had dropped off their son without clothes for the weekend. After taking 15 minutes to explain how self-centered and irresponsible she was, he demanded that I file an emergency motion asking that she be told by the court to provide clothes for the weekends. I calmly reminded him that this call had cost him more than if he had gone to Kmart and bought a few items. Hint: If your spouse drops your child off without a pair of sneakers for the weekend, do yourself a favor and don't call your lawyer.

TAKE THE HIGH ROAD.

No matter what your former spouse is saying about you, no matter how terrible of a partner they might have been during the marriage, take the high road—at least when your kids are around. Children who are products of amicable divorces do better in school, have higher self-esteem and are generally more successful. Work together for the benefit of your children.

Day 26 Exercise

Get a calendar to schedule key dates. First, obtain your children's school calendar and mark all of the holidays, days off and vacations on it. Decide which days you want and which days your spouse will get. Bring this to your meeting when you negotiate the parenting plan. Figure out which days you agree upon and work on developing a plan for the rest of the days. Prepare a year-long plan that can be repeated or reworked each year.

Day 26 Meditation/Affirmation

"I am an excellent parent. I place my children's needs first and will develop a plan that serves their best interests."

Day 27

CHILD SUPPORT

SMH = "shaking my head." I have an SMH story about child support. Linda and Keith were negotiating their divorce settlement. Linda, 42, was a nurse who had immigrated to America to marry Keith. Keith, 63, was a small business owner. Together, they had a 13-year-old daughter. After a long and intense day of mediation, they finally reached an agreement. The agreement, typed and ready to sign, was reviewed by Linda and Keith and their attorneys. Linda, satisfied that the terms accurately reflected their agreement, initialed each page and signed the last line. The agreement was then to be signed by Keith.

When he came upon the "child support" section, Keith exploded out of his seat and exclaimed, "What is this? You mean I will have to pay child support until I am 68 years old?! That's absolutely absurd! I won't do it!" He began packing up his papers and started to leave. But before Keith made his exit, the flabbergasted mediator responded by stating the obvious: "Well, who told you to have a child when you were 50?" SMH.

Child support must be paid by parents to provide for the children's needs and it continues until a child is 18 years of age (or until they graduate from high school in some states). The obligation to support the children can legally cease if the teen becomes emancipated by getting married, joining the military, or declaring emancipation.

Parents have to support their children; state governments do not want to take the responsibility for it. Therefore, the states have created elaborate plans to ensure that they have taken every measure possible to make parents support their own children. States figure out, based upon the parents' incomes, how much they should be spending on their children. Therefore, in most states, child support is based on the combined gross income of the two parents. The next part of the equation is determining how much time the children spend with each parent. Other variables also can be part of the equation, such as health insurance premiums and daycare costs. Most states have guidelines, so once the numbers are plugged into the formula, a number is calculated—and that's what has to be paid.

Because of the guidelines, this can be a simpler area of the law; however, there is one variable that can complicate the matter: income. Sometimes, determining the parties' incomes is the most challenging part. Salaried income from a job is transparent, of course. But if one of the spouses owns their own business, income may come in the form of benefits, such as car and cellphone payments. The business might pick up the tab for restaurant bills, travel and other perquisites. In this case, coming to an agreement on the true income can be a challenge.

Income also can be dividend income that one party is receiving on investments or alimony. Income is any form of a continuous stream of payments expected to persist. Therefore, if your parents regularly give you money and the other side can prove that this is expected to continue, that might be classified as income.

And then there's the Catch-22 twist. Income that you aren't receiving can be characterized as income. How can that be? If you aren't working, or you aren't working to your potential as far as earnings, the court has the discretion to "declare" that you are earning more—even if you are not! And child support can be based on that phantom number. For example, Suzi was a lawyer earning $100,000 per year at a large law firm. Dissatisfied with her career, she quit her job and followed her passion by opening a flower shop. One year after opening her shop, she filed for divorce from Joey, who had been laid off from his position as a welder. Despite his best efforts, Joey was only able to find a job making minimum wage as a clerk at Walmart. Her income last year was $45,000 and his was $21,000. Joey's lawyer argued that Suzi was "voluntarily underemployed" because she could go back into the practice of law and earn far more annually. The court agreed and imputed the income of $100,000 per year to her. Joey's income, on the other hand, was $50,000 annually as a welder. Because he had proven to the court that he had put forth his best efforts to replace that job but couldn't, there was no imputation of extra income to him. Under this scenario, the child support calculation would be computed with Suzi making $100,000 (even though she wasn't actually making this) and Joey making $21,000. (Imputation of income also can take place in an alimony calculation, by the way.)

In divorce, it's not uncommon to hear a litany of stories about why someone isn't earning their full potential, such as that the husband will be retiring at 51 years old or that his once-successful business has tanked with no forecast of recovery, or that the stay-at-home wife doesn't have job skills or experience. The list is endless. Each side may attempt to create the bleakest possible picture in order to avoid paying what they perceive to be excessive support. To discourage this sort of manipulation, the courts created the imputation mechanism to hold parents responsible for supporting their children.

Courts can rule to deviate from guidelines from time to time. In Florida, there was a famous case involving a basketball player from the Orlando Magic. Because his income was so high, the mother was receiving astronomical child support payments. Rather than allow her to be enriched beyond what was needed for their child's support, the court ordered that she would receive a portion for support and the balance would be placed in a trust for the future benefit of the child. Another reason to deviate would be in the case of a special needs child who requires costly educational enrichment, medication or regular medical care.

Generally, child support can be adjusted at any time. If your former spouse has moved into a $20 million crib on the beach, then you might want to petition the court to consider whether the current child support payments should be modified. Also, if your children are spending more time with you than what was contemplated under the parenting plan and you are the payer, you might want to ask for a change in payments. Remember, if you don't tell the court what is going on, then the last order always stands as accurate. It is highly unlikely that your spouse will admit that you have overpaid and that you should be given a refund because the child has been living with you. It is incumbent on you to take affirmative action to make a change or correction.

Alert! Child support is not to be messed with. States take this very seriously. If you don't pay, your paycheck can be garnished, a lien can be placed on your home, or you could lose your driver's license or professional license. Even worse, you can be jailed. Also, child support is not dischargeable in a bankruptcy. If you think you are overpaying, go in front a judge immediately and let the court know why.

What is not covered under child support, but usually must be determined, are uncovered medical expenses, extracurricular activities and college expenses. There is a very important distinction between a *statutory obligation* (meaning the state can make you) and a *contractual obligation* (meaning you signed up to do this and the court can enforce your promise). Child support is a statutory obligation. Parents cannot waive this obligation. It is the law. Payments for uncovered medical expenses, extracurricular activities and college are not statutory. Courts generally will not make a parent pay for college. However, if you sign a marital settlement agreement which says you will pay for half of the college expenses, then the court will enforce your contractual obligation and make you pay. Many times, parents will use the ratios of their incomes for these obligations. In other words, if the husband is making 60 percent of the income and the wife is making 40 percent, they will share in the other obligations using the same ratio.

Day 27 Exercise

Figure out what your gross income should be. Include all revenue streams. If your spouse is not sticking to the parenting plan, keep a detailed log of visitations. This will be very helpful if you decide to ask the court for a revised plan. Determine what the costs are for your children's health insurance premiums and how much you spend out of pocket annually for uncovered medical expenses. Finally, determine exactly how much you spend per month for your children's extracurricular activities.

Day 27 Meditation/Affirmation

"I will provide for my children and they will be supported in such a way that all of their needs are met."

Day 28

OTHER ISSUES

SEXUALLY TRANSMITTED DISEASE

Jennifer was perplexed when she discovered that she had sores around her genital area. An examination by her gynecologist revealed the shocking diagnosis: genital herpes. She knew that she had never been unfaithful to David, her husband of 20 years, and that he was the only man with whom she had ever had sexual relations. Still dressed in the paper gown, perched on the examination table, a second shock wave suddenly came over her. Her husband must have been unfaithful and given her an incurable sexually transmitted disease.

The statistics are staggering. The Centers for Disease Control estimates that 776,000 people are diagnosed with genital herpes each year. In fact, nearly 50 million are estimated to be infected with herpes simplex virus 2 (the genital variety). The other dismal news is that transmission is more likely to take place from male to female, which means that many more women are infected than men. As large as the infected population is, it does little to assuage the feeling of being kicked in the stomach upon learning that you have become one of those statistics.

In divorce, sexually transmitted diseases can carry their own claim as an interspousal tort. A tort is a civil wrongdoing by one person which causes another person loss, pain or damages. If a spouse believes a sexually transmitted disease has been contracted from the other spouse, a claim for battery or negligence can be made. In this sort of claim, the wronged spouse would either claim that the other spouse transmitted a disease on purpose (knew about it but didn't tell their spouse) or should have known and should be held accountable. These civil claims are litigated along with the other divorce issues. The damages are usually in the form of payment for medicine, medical care or psychiatric treatment.

However, these types of cases are very difficult to prove. Who is to say that Jennifer didn't cheat and give it to David? How does one prove that? How long is the incubation period? Is it possible that David was unknowingly infected prior the marriage and it had just become active? For these sorts of reasons—although salacious and embarrassing—these cases usually settle before ever getting into the courtroom.

"REVEALERS"

Not as common, but equally as incendiary, is when one of the parties comes out as gay, lesbian, cross-dressing or transgendered. These are considered "revealers." These are very delicate matters in which both parties experience excruciating pain and suffering. The revealer has struggled with this self-knowledge for years. For the party to whom this information has been revealed, the whole world is stripped away in one fell swoop. When children are involved, it becomes much more delicate.

When children are involved, the impulse might be to take the children away from the revealer. Fear instigates the reaction to take flight and run, but take your time. Both parties should seek professional assistance and include the children. Your emotions will range from shock, anger, devastation and revulsion to hurt and betrayal. If you are not the revealer, remember that this is not your fault. While you may feel betrayed, this is not a reflection of you. You cannot control or change the situation.

Establish a well thought out and organized plan. Is the revealer causing any harm to your children? Or is this the same person you have always known—now in a new light? Trying to take your children away could actually cause more damage to your former spouse or children. Courts will weigh what is in the best interest of the children. Living a particular lifestyle that differs from the norm is not inherently the death knell for a parent. Take the time to breathe and ascertain your motivations. What is genuinely best for the children? Do not to use the children as a sword to punish the other person.

Day 28 Exercise

Write a letter to your spouse today to explain every emotion you are feeling and why. When it's done, read it and decide if that is how you still feel. If you left something out, add it. If you wrote something down that you no longer feel, then delete it. Don't give the letter to your spouse. Take it outside and burn it. While you do so, give your feelings to the universe. Decide that your negative emotions, along with the letter, are going up in smoke.

Day 28 Meditation/Affirmation

"I will transform this event in my life into one that is positive and gives me strength."

Day 29

PROCEDURE

Having spent the most of the year working in Argentina, Louis was looking forward to returning home for Christmas and spending it with his wife of 23 years and his two sons while they were home from college. It was Christmas Eve. He boarded the plane, barely noticing that the flight attendants were wearing red Santa hats and serving egg nog. He relaxed back into his seat, reflecting on the difficulties he and Sara had been having. She had made it clear that she was unhappy in the marriage, but the demands of his career commanded his undivided attention. Still, he believed she was a good wife and devoted mother, and he was contentedly anticipating their time together.

The plane landed in Fort Lauderdale on schedule and he looked out the window to see the palm trees greeting the plane. He grabbed his carry-on and disembarked. As he made his way down the gate, he was distracted in his thoughts, when suddenly a gentleman dressed in a polo shirt and khakis approached him. "Louis Averman?" "Mr. Louis Averman?" Startled, Louis turned away and his pace quickened. Determined, the gentleman kept pace with him and began to hand him a package of documents. "A lawsuit has been filed against you. You have been served," the stranger explained. Clutching the documents, a dazed Louis watched as the gentleman disappeared into the crowd.

When he finally gathered himself, Louis read the first page. Sara had filed for divorce. She had served him with a Petition for Dissolution of Marriage which she had filed with the clerk of court. He had 20 days to answer the petition or the court could file a default judgment against him for failure to answer and Sara would get what she had requested.

While not always dramatic, this is how a divorce procedure begins. When you meet with your lawyer for the first time, you will be asked a series of questions. Be prepared to detail the history of your marriage, your family, your financial details and details about the children. Your lawyer will explain the law to you. Equally important as the law is understanding the procedure of the case or the process.

When you decide to file, your lawyer will give you a list of documents that you will need to pull together so that you can provide financial information (also known as financial disclosure) to the other side. It will include the information we talked about on Day 21. Both sides will provide this information to each other. This helps the judge determine the "his," "hers" and "theirs" piles. Once the information has been exchanged then you are prepared to negotiate a settlement. This can be done at any time during the case, but your lawyers are not likely to be comfortable having settlement discussions until there is a true accounting of the financial picture.

When you resolve your case, you are done. There might be final paperwork to complete, but for all intents and purposes, you are close to being divorced. If you haven't resolved your case, you proceed to mediation. Some jurisdictions specifically require family law cases to be mediated. If you settle the case in mediation (and we will discuss mediation in greater detail at Day 34) then you are done. If you don't, then you go into a courtroom for the trial (or final hearing) to explain to a judge what hasn't been resolved. Whether you are ready or not, the judge will issue a decision after hearing the case, and the case will be settled.

Your lawyer will draft the petition (sometimes called a complaint) and will draft a summons. Once the petition and summons are served upon your spouse, it needs to be answered in 20 or 30 days. The petition is a critical document because it tells the court what you want. You will request everything you might possibly want down the road. You must include everything you can think of because you cannot be granted relief for items which you do not originally request. In other words, if you end up standing before the judge at the end of the divorce process and state that you want alimony, but failed to ask for it in your petition or complaint, your request will likely be denied. For that reason, expect your spouse to file a counter-petition or counter-complaint and prepare to steel yourself. Your spouse will be asking for everything that might be desired down the road, too, so don't freak out. Expect that it will be upsetting to you, then take a deep breath and move on.

Once the petition or complaint is filed, you have an active case open with the court. Now, within your case, you can move (or ask) the court to issue orders on your behalf during the pendency of the case. For example, you may want to file a Motion for Temporary Relief. In this type of motion, you will ask the court to order your spouse to do certain things during the time the case is open, such as pay certain bills, temporary support or attorney's fees. You might also ask for a temporary parenting schedule or temporary child support. Once a motion is filed, your attorney will have to set the motion for a hearing in front of the judge. At the hearing, your attorney will explain to the judge the reasons why you should be granted the relief you are seeking.

Divorce is like pregnancy. In order to get to the end result, you have to go through certain stages, some more painful than others. None of the ways to the end are particularly easy. Just as some women have problem-free births, some couples resolve their differences with minimal conflict, but there are still periods of pain.

Others endure excruciating and lengthy suffering to get to their end result. Either way, the end result is divorce. Staying focused on the fact that you are heading toward your new life will make the process a whole lot more palatable.

Day 29 Exercise

Gather the following information for your attorney to draft the initial documents:

1. Your full name
2. Your spouse's full name
3. Your date of birth
4. Your spouse's date of birth
5. Your Social Security number
6. Your spouse's Social Security number
7. Your date of marriage
8. Your place of marriage
9. The full names of your children
10. Your children's birthdates
11. The addresses where your children have resided for the past three years
12. Your employer and income
13. Your spouse's employer and income
14. A copy of your driver's license or other proof of residence in your state
15. The full addresses of all real estate which you will be requesting the court to order to be sold
16. A copy of a prenuptial agreement or other agreements between you and your spouse
17. Copies of any orders or injunctions related to domestic violence

Day 29 Meditation/Affirmation

"Gathering this information continues to empower and center me. I am immovable from my center of balance."

Day 30

INJUNCTIONS

Don't come near me! Don't waste our money! Don't cut me out of your will! Sound familiar? These are phrases that might be angrily uttered during the course of divorce proceedings. How can you prevent these kinds of things? Through an injunction. An injunction, sometimes called a restraining order, is a court order prohibiting specific actions. These are often requested in emergency or urgent situations during a divorce. There are two important ones to understand.

DOMESTIC VIOLENCE INJUNCTIONS

If your spouse is violent, threatening or stalking you in such a way that you fear for you safety, then you can request that the court enter a domestic violence injunction. You will have to go to your local law enforcement agency and fill out documents and draft a sworn statement about why you want this protection. Sometimes courts will examine the information and make a decision to enter the order *ex parte* until a hearing can be held. *Ex parte* means that without the other person's knowledge or participation in the process, the court simply enters the order. However, constitutional rights provide that people have the right to have notice and an opportunity to be heard. Therefore, if the injunction is issued *ex parte* then a hearing will be hastily scheduled to ascertain whether the injunction should be upheld.

If you find yourself at a hearing, whether you are the recipient of the injunction or you requested it, be prepared. Hire a lawyer if you can. Going into these types of hearings is legal suicide without a lawyer. Have your evidence and witnesses ready to go. Regardless of which side you are on, your future will be altered by the outcome of this hearing. If you have requested the hearing, you will have good reason to fear retribution if you lose. If you are the recipient of the injunction, the prospect of the court extending it on a permanent basis will mean a permanent record of domestic violence. There could be long-term implications for you with current or future employment. Take this very, very seriously.

One very important distinction to understand is the difference between a permanent domestic violence injunction and a civil no-contact order. To demonstrate the critical difference, I offer a horror story. Claire was married to a wealthy young investor, Zach, who had made his first $5 million before he turned 30. Handsome, brilliant and rich, she fell for him instantly and they were married three months after they met. Within the first three years of marriage, they were the parents of two young children. Soon after the marriage, Claire discovered that Zach had been treated for bipolar disorder for several years. She suspected that he also used illicit drugs but wasn't sure. After the birth of their second child, he decided he no longer liked the way the medications were making him feel, so he stopped taking them cold turkey. He immediately became abusive. After several incidents, she moved into her mother's home and immediately filed a Petition for Domestic Violence Injunction. The injunction was granted *ex parte* and the hearing was set.

At the hearing, before appearing before the judge, Zach's attorney approached Claire's attorney to discuss a possible settlement. Claire's attorney assured her that the injunction would remain in place. She also negotiated a few other items. They then represented to the judge that an agreement had been reached. Upon receiving the order, she learned for the first time that her attorney had agreed to dismiss the order of domestic violence injunction and had agreed to exchange it for a civil no-contact order. The key difference lies in the remedy for enforcement. With a civil order, the remedy for enforcement is through the courts, as if a contract has been breached. The remedy for violation of a domestic violence injunction is calling the police and having the perpetrator shipped off to jail. Big difference.

FINANCIAL INJUNCTIONS

The other type of injunction centers on financial issues. Sometimes courts will issue automatic orders (also called Standing Orders) during the filing of the petition or complaint. These will basically state that you can spend your money as you did prior to the filing in the normal course of business, but you may not make large, sudden movements. For instance, you can't sell or dispose of property without the written consent of the other party or an order from the court allowing it.

If you are concerned that your spouse will drain a bank account, rack up credit card debt, or send large sums of marital funds overseas, you can request that the court issue an *ex parte* order to freeze the accounts. As with the domestic violence injunction, the court will hold a hearing in short order. Getting these orders entered *ex parte* is not always easy. Be prepared to prove there is imminent danger of dissipation of the assets; otherwise, the court may not be inclined to grant it without the benefit of hearing the other side of the story.

PLAN AHEAD

These orders are reactive in nature. One person's behavior causes the other person to run interference by obtaining a court order to try to prevent certain activity. While injunctions can certainly be effective, planning ahead and taking offensive measures can often be even more effective. Sometimes, having a conversation with your banker or financial representative at the time of filing can result in the same relief without having to take drastic measures in court. Financial institutions loathe being inserted in erupting divorce conflict. Often times, if an institution is alerted of a potential issue, it will place a hold or freeze on particular accounts. Both parties are then required to execute written consent before any withdrawals of funds are allowed.

Planning ahead in domestic violence situations is a bit tougher. If you are living in an explosive situation, find out your options. Go back to Day 8 of this book and be certain you are prepared.

Keep in mind the old saying, "If you stay ready, you don't have to get ready."

Day 30 Exercise

If you are concerned about your spouse potentially wasting or dissipating marital assets, contact your financial institutions about placing a hold or freeze on joint accounts, including credit cards. The other action you can take is a bit more drastic but effective if you are truly concerned. Go to your financial institution and withdraw half of the value of the joint accounts and place them into an account with your own name. Choose a different financial institution to open your new account to avoid ownership confusion when your irate spouse shows up at the banker's door. By taking only half of the value, you are showing good faith if you have to explain your actions later to a judge.

Day 30 Meditation/Affirmation

"I am prepared and I have the courage to take the steps necessary to walk toward my new life."

Day 31

DISCOVERY

Do you want to know if your spouse has a hidden bank account? Would you like to pore over credit card statements to scrutinize whether your spouse has spent money on a paramour?

Discovery is the process in divorce of gathering that sort of information. Wending your way through miles of bank, credit card and earnings statements, tax returns and other financial documents is part of the process.

In divorce, both sides have to disclose all of their financial information. This will include the statements listed above as well as copies of deeds to real estate, titles to automobiles, boats, copies of life insurance policies and statements, and proof of loan balances. A lot of time is spent in this phase of a divorce. In order to settle a case with a comfort level that the resolution is based upon full disclosure, the discovery must be complete.

Here is where a divorce can get expensive. If you and your spouse dicker over the values of everything, the only way to come to a resolution is through appraisals—which cost money. If you or your spouse refuse to cooperate with the other side or with the court by willingly producing the appropriate documents, the recourse is to file motions asking the court to make the other side behave—which gets costly. If one party is hiding assets and the other hires an asset search company to find the assets—this, too, will also cost lots of money.

VALUATION ISSUES

A major hurdle in the discovery process can be agreeing to valuations of particular assets. Real estate, furniture, jewelry and other hard assets can be appraised fairly easily. Even so, these types of appraisals can get costly if a spouse doesn't agree with the appraised values. Furniture can be a real hot button because it does not hold its value. People are often shocked and insulted to learn that the furniture for which they paid $100,000 is now worth pennies on the dollar.

More complicated are valuations of businesses. If one or both spouses started a business during the marriage then the businesses have marital value. Gathering the information to complete that evaluation can be a challenge. Sometimes, the books may be incomplete or in disarray. Confidentiality issues also can stonewall the process, which can be rectified by executing confidentiality agreements. Most of the time, these kinds of valuations are performed by an outside expert, such as a forensic accountant who has expertise in valuing businesses. The forensic accountant will testify in court about the findings. If you hire one, your spouse will most likely hire one to refute the testimony of your expert. (Can you hear the cha-ching sound? That is the sound of a divorce becoming increasingly expensive, although bringing in these types of experts is often unavoidable.)

CHILDREN'S ISSUES

Clara had accused Jeff of exposing the children to sexual websites and other inappropriate material around the house. She also asserted that she had been the primary caregiver, so she should have more timesharing with the children. Claiming that Jeff had never participated in helping the children with their homework or attending a parent-teacher conference, she fought hard to besmirch Jeff as a parent. Jeff, on the other hand, claimed that Clara was unstable and was doing illicit drugs.

He also asserted that he had been the primary caregiver, claiming that Clara sometimes failed to feed the children dinner or give them evening baths. The court, exasperated and confused, ordered a parenting evaluation to help with its decision about what parenting arrangement would be in the best interest of the children.

If there is a particularly acrimonious situation between parents and they are accusing each other of all sorts of sordid behaviors, the court can order a custody evaluation (sometimes called a parenting evaluation). A psychologist who is trained to perform these types of evaluations is appointed by the court. The psychologist will interview pertinent individuals in the children's lives. They often visit the homes, schools and other places where the children spend a significant amount of time. This professional can perform psychological testing on the parents and may request that they submit to drug testing.

In effect, the psychologist becomes the gatherer of information for the court. After the written report is published, the evaluator will testify in court regarding their report and the information they gathered. The court often relies on the opinions of the parenting evaluator because the psychologist is viewed as a neutral party who is rendering a professional opinion based on firsthand observations.

INCOME ISSUES

Kate had been a stay-at-home mom for 20 years but before she "retired" to become a mommy, she had a law degree and had practiced for a few years prior to and during the early years of the marriage. Dennis knew that Kate was very bright and highly organized. Kate had no desire to return to the workforce. Dennis wanted very much to limit her alimony claim. To combat her claim that she wasn't able to earn a wage, he asked the court to appoint a vocational rehabilitative expert to perform an evaluation on Kate.

These kinds of experts perform testing on the subject person. They also do research to determine how long it would take to rehabilitate the person, how that could be done (being quite specific about what educational institution they would have to attend and how much it would be), and what the demand is in the current market for that type of position. These evaluators sometimes contact local employers to determine if there are openings and how much they would pay for a new hire with a particular background. This type of expert also prepares a written report and can testify as to their findings in court if necessary.

WAYS TO DISCOVER INFORMATION

In divorce, there is a certain amount of information that has to be exchanged automatically. If it is determined that that information is insufficient, there are several other modes of discovery. First, your lawyer can send a Request to Produce on your behalf. In that request, you will ask for whatever documents you want. The other side will then have 20 or 30 days to get the documents back to you. The rub here is that the request has to have a reasonable connection to your situation. If you ask for complete bank statements dating back to 1972, you will probably get a Motion for Protective Order as your response. A Motion for Protective Order is a motion asking for the court's protection from this request. You will then proceed down to the courthouse and explain why you need the information you requested and the court will make a determination as to whether you will get it. The court can narrow the scope and grant your request in part and deny it in part.

Another method of gathering information is through interrogatories. These are written questions that you send to the other side. The soon-to-be Ex answers them and signs a statement swearing that the responses are truthful. Because these are sworn, if the responding party is not truthful, these untruths can rear their ugly head in the form of impeachment at future hearings or at trial. If your answers are inconsistent with responses you give in later depositions or hearings, you will hear about it. Bottom line: Don't guess and don't lie. Answer the questions as honestly as you can.

Depositions are another way lawyers gather information. The party that is being deposed shows up in person to answer questions under oath with a court reporter present to take down every word. Anyone involved in the case can be called for a deposition: you, your spouse or a forensic accountant. Generally, any question that will lead admissible evidence at trial can be asked. Your lawyer will object if the question delves into uncomfortable territory (such as attorney-client privilege) or the questions are clearly designed to harass the deponent.

In your deposition, tell the truth, but don't be too chatty. Volunteering too much information might come back to bite you later. Do not guess. Also, make sure that your responses are verbal as the court reporter cannot take down nods or shakes of the head.

Day 31 Exercise

Journal your goals for the case. State what your overall plan is and think about what's required to get that done. Your attorney can help you with this part.

For example:

- Let my spouse keep the business (need financial documentation and valuation)
- Sell the marital home (don't need appraisal)
- I want to keep the marital home (need an appraisal)
- Impute income to spouse who hasn't worked in 20 years (need evaluation)
- Both parties work and will keep current positions (don't need evaluation)
- Implement agreed-upon parenting plan (on evaluation needed)

Day 31 Meditation/Affirmation

"With confidence and courage, I am taking positive actions to bring positive results into my life."

Day 32

FACEBOOK

There may be a new breed of home-wrecker in town—and it isn't who you might think. Some experts are now decrying Facebook for more reasons than its volatile stock value.

BY THE NUMBERS

81%—This is the percentage of the nation's top divorce lawyers who have reported that their clients blame social media for the demise of their marriage, according to a study released recently by the American Academy of Matrimonial Lawyers. 33%—This is the percentage, according to a recent ABC News poll, of all divorce filings last year which contained the word Facebook. 66%—This is the percentage of people who have cited Facebook as their primary source of online divorce evidence.

The Centers for Disease Control (CDC) releases the statistics each year for both the marriage rates and the divorce rates. In 2010, the CDC reported that 3.6 of every 1,000 people were divorced and that 6.8 out of every 1,000 were married. The conclusion that can be drawn is that the divorce rate continues to hover at 50 percent, which is what most people suspect and believe. It is interesting to note that while the population continues to boom, the divorce rate has slightly declined over the past few years, but so has the rate of marriage.

What may come as a surprise is that the rate of divorce in America dramatically differs depending upon what number the marriage is. While it's commonly noted that half of all marriages end in divorce, that rate applies to *first* marriages. Indeed, the more times that one marries, the worse the chances are of success. 60% of second marriages and 73% of third marriages fail.

SOCIAL MEDIA

While Facebook has been lauded as a convenient way to keep in touch with family and friends, it has brought a whole new meaning to the phrase "bringing people together." In my divorce law practice, I have filed several cases in the past year in which my clients have pointed the blame at Facebook for the spouse's new paramour and the demise of the marriage. In the cases I have seen, it is usually an old flame—usually a former college sweetheart or an unrequited high school crush. And apparently the flame can flicker for a lifetime, as I have witnessed instances of couples in their 70s reconnecting with a past love when more than 50 years have gone by since their last encounter.

Many experts have said that it usually starts off innocently. A spouse is curious about what may have happened with a former boyfriend or girlfriend and begin exchanging dialogue about their lives, children and careers. Prior to social media and the boom of cellphones, it was not uncommon for people to lose track of one another once their lives diverged. Staying in touch took more effort. It required a commitment to write letters and was expensive to make long-distance telephone calls.

Today, connecting is as easy as hitting send on the Facebook "friend request" button. The flip side, of course, is that extramarital affairs, once stealth and covert operations, exist in an entirely different realm. Due to the rapid-fire nature of social media, cheating spouses are far more likely to get caught. Everyone becomes a potential private investigator, from the spouse or a brother-in-law to neighbors and co-workers. Salacious romance details and suggestive photographs are sure to be noticed and shared.

PROTECTING YOURSELF

Some marriage counselors have completely condemned all social media and suggest a self-imposed ban for all married couples. A more moderate approach may be prudent. If you choose to participate in social media, make sure that anything you post is something you wouldn't mind being projected on a white board for everyone in a courtroom to see. Mind your Ps and Qs. If someone takes a drunken, naked picture of you when you're out partying one night, no doubt these unflattering gems will be posted on Facebook and tagged with your name for all the world to see. Be on your best behavior in the months leading up to and during the divorce to save yourself a lot of grief.

Day 32 Exercise

Check out your Facebook page. Make sure that there are no posts or pictures that are compromising. If there are, delete them. Check your privacy settings and be sure they are at the highest protection level. (And don't rest on your laurels. Facebook privacy walls can be broken or breached.) Delete your Facebook account for the pendency of the divorce if you are concerned. Remember: Do not post anything online that you wouldn't want to see on a huge poster board in court.

Day 32 Meditation/Affirmation

"I am taking responsibility for my online activities because I know it will lead to my ideal life."

Day 33

NEGOTIATION

Your palms are sweating and your heart is pounding. Is it because you are at your seventh-grade dance? No, it's because you are getting ready to negotiate your alimony payments or a parenting plan for your kids. Many of us feel completely confident going to bat on behalf of their children, friends or family. But when it comes to advocating for ourselves, we stumble and crumble.

Approaching the negotiation process is an essential skill. We constantly negotiate in our daily lives—in real estate, business, work, marriage and family. This is where the gender gap rears its ugly head. Generally men are more confident in negotiating than women. There is a psychology behind that. In her book *Lean In: Women, Work and the Will to Lead*, Sheryl Sandberg tells a compelling story about Howard and Heidi. In that story, business school students were broken up into two groups. Both groups read a success story about a person who became a successful venture capitalist through their skill and outgoing personality. Both groups were asked to rate the appeal of the protagonist and conclude whether the subject was a likable person who they would want to hire. The stories were identical, except one was about a woman named Heidi and the other one was about a man named Howard. The students praised Howard, deeming him a likable person they would want on their team. Heidi did not fare so well. The group found her selfish and unlikable—not the type of person they would want to work for or hire. Same story—with a change in names and pronouns. Women are probably less confident in negotiating because they want to be liked and they innately know that if they come on too strong, they may not be viewed as likable.

I FEEL CONFIDENT

Ultimately, Sheryl Sandberg, Facebook Chief Operating Officer, shares in her book that Mark Zuckerberg, her much younger boss, told her that her desire to be liked was holding her back. In divorce, winning a popularity contest is not the goal. Achieving an equitable result is the goal. Approach your negotiations with confidence. Begin building your confidence long before you enter into real-time negotiations. Know your topic inside and out. Prepare yourself physically. Choose an outfit that you love and know you look fabulous in. When you feel great, you shine.

PREPARATION IS THE KEY

Having all of the discovery completed is one way to prepare. It is also critical to know the other side's position and why they may have taken that position. Be ready to address any points they may have. It is also important to have a range for your best-case scenario and worst-case scenario. Know the strengths and weaknesses of your argument. Before going in, establish your "choke point"—the point at which you will stand up and walk away with your dignity fully intact.

DURING THE NEGOTIATION PROCESS

Take a list of what you want into the negotiation. Ask for a lot and expect less. Be aware of the triggers that cause you to become upset. Keeping your emotions in check and remaining calm is essential in maintaining control of the overall process. Present yourself as no-nonsense, confident and matter-of-fact. Do not ever appear as pleading, worried or intimidated, even if your knees are knocking as you walk in.

Know your value and stand your ground for it. Prepare a summary of your first offer and your next offer so that you have it to reference during negotiations (for yourself, not to share with the other side). Be as specific as you can be. Present your side with no apologies, from a position of strength. Think about it like this: Quality people are essential to a successful business, so you may be more valuable to your company than the company is to you.

Before you leave the table, be sure to memorialize your agreement in writing and get it signed.

AND FINALLY

Ultimately, trust your gut. If it feels wrong, it probably is wrong. Do not agree because you don't want to make waves, you don't want someone to be mad at you, or worst of all, because they harassed you into it and you just want it to be over. Don't agree to something unless you instinctively know that it is the absolute best and right thing for you. You will regret it immediately and the resentment will gnaw and fester, robbing you of the closure you were seeking.

In every moment, you alone have the power to decide what your reality is and will be. And remember: Others will only value you to the level that you value yourself.

Day 33 Exercise

Prepare a first offer and a next offer. Then determine your worst-case scenario and your choke point. Discuss these options with your attorney to be certain they are reasonable in the eyes of the law.

Day 33 Meditation/Affirmation

"I am seizing the moment to honor my commitment to myself to resolve this case so that I can continue creating my new life."

Day 34

MEDIATION

If you knew that something was highly effective at saving you a lot of money and bringing peace to your life, would you do it? Mediation can do that for you. A form of alternative dispute resolution, mediation is a private process in which you and your spouse participate with your attorneys. A neutral third-party mediator is hired to assist you in reaching a resolution. The mediator is usually a lawyer who has been trained in dispute resolution. The mediator (unlike in arbitration) has no decision-making authority but will help facilitate a resolution between you and your spouse.

BEFORE MEDIATION

Before mediation, you will meet with your attorney and go over the process. You also will discuss the pros and cons of your case and potential outcomes if you go to trial. This is when you and your attorney also discuss the summaries of your best-case and worst-case scenarios.

DURING MEDIATION

Generally, mediation starts in the same room. The mediator will give you and your spouse an overview and your attorneys will be present, too. Other professionals may attend, such as your forensic accountants. Do not plan on bringing along friends or family members unless you feel you simply cannot function without them. Your spouse can object to their participation and you may end up working against yourself by bringing people along who will impede the process. For example, don't take your brother because you think he intimidates your husband.

The mediator's overview might go like this:

"Today is your day of opportunity. An opportunity to settle your case privately and to have control over the outcome. If you go to trial, the courtrooms are open to the public and anyone can walk in and hear details about your private life. Furthermore, the judge will render a decision that neither of you could like. Plus, it will cost you lots and lots of money in attorney's fees to properly prepare for trial. If you want your case settled today, we can get it done. There are several creative ways to resolve issues."

Your lawyers can provide an overview of the case and the outstanding issues to the mediator. You will be asked to sign an agreement with the mediator. Then you will probably be split into separate rooms, which is called caucusing. The mediator will move back and forth between the two rooms and present offers until the case is settled or until you declare an impasse.

TWO LAYERS OF CONFIDENTIALITY

There are two layers of confidentiality in mediation. The first layer is on the entire mediation process. The court system is clogged and courts want the process to work so there are less pending cases. One way to facilitate this is by declaring that the mediation process is confidential. Therefore, if you or your spouse makes an offer in good faith in an attempt to settle the case, the other party can't announce at trial that you would have settled for x. If that was a risk, nobody would offer anything. The second layer of confidentiality is between you and the mediator. You and your attorney can share information or a strategy with the mediator that you can ask the mediator not to share.

AGREEMENT

Make sure you get a written agreement signed that day. There is no buyer's remorse in any field like there is in family law. All the time, people second-guess their decisions. You will wake up the next day feeling like you gave away too much or didn't fight hard enough in a certain area. By signing an agreement, you can be sure that part of the case is done.

You can also settle parts of cases in mediation. Perhaps you come to an agreement on the property settlement but not the alimony, so you sign an agreement on the property settlement then go to court to ask the judge to rule on alimony. Do yourself a favor and give the mediation process a chance to work. Showing up with a chip on your shoulder that you aren't going to stay for more than an hour is unproductive. Be prepared to be cooperative and reasonable.

Day 34 Exercise

Talk to your attorney about which mediators are the best ones in your area and research their backgrounds. Review the mediation agreement ahead of time with your attorney. Meet with your attorney prior to the day of mediation.

Day 34 Meditation/Affirmation

"I harmoniously resolve conflicts for my own good and the good of my family."

Day 35

TRIAL

Well, so much for that amicable divorce you thought you were going to have. You've tried to settle it yourselves and you even went to mediation. Alas, none of those options worked so you're off to trial. Instead of a divorce trial, I irreverently refer to it as the "divorce gamble" because that calls a spade a spade. If you go before the judge, you will not get justice. You will get a decision. That decision will be based upon the judge. Judges are human. Humans make mistakes. That is why there is an appeals process. However, if you and your spouse simply cannot come to a meeting of the mind, there will be one last stop on your journey to freedom, and this time the shore excursion will be to the courthouse.

TRIAL PREPARATION

The majority of this will be done by your lawyer. Why are trials so expensive? A short list of what your lawyer will have to do to prepare might look like this:

Create financial exhibits.

Create any other types of exhibits.

Create summaries of bank statements.

Create a timeline of the events.

Research legal issues, find case law and possibly draft a memorandum of law.

Review any memoranda of law written by the other side and find cases which refute their position.

Review depositions taken in the case and summarize them.

Review evaluations performed in the case.

Review all of the documents produced in the case.

Review medical or psychological records.

Prepare an opening statement.

Prepare direct examinations of all witnesses.

Discuss the direct examination with all witnesses.

Prepare cross-examinations of all witnesses.

Categorize all exhibits into a trial notebook.

Prepare last-minute motions which should be heard prior to trial.

Prepare a closing argument.

These tasks add up to hours and hours and hours of work, but they are necessary in order to be properly prepared.

Prior to the day of trial, the lawyers for both sides can agree that certain documents will be admitted as evidence, which saves time at trial.

THE BIG DAY

On the day of trial, please dress appropriately. Ladies, that short, sexy skirt will not sway the male judge. No jeans and nothing revealing. A nice dress or blouse and dress pants. Guys, wear a button-down, long-sleeve shirt and khakis at a *minimum*. For both guys and gals, suits are always a good choice. Do not bring your children into the courtroom.

Your demeanor should be respectful. No eye-rolling, loud sighs or disruptive outbursts. Maintain your composure. I had a client who I will call Laura who made a huge mistake. During a hearing on *her* motion for contempt because her ex-husband wasn't paying alimony, we ran out of time. The judge expressed his regret, but went out of his way to schedule our case the following week. I thanked the judge and began packing up when what do my wondering ears hear? A voice exclaim very loudly, "This is *preposterous!*" To my dismay, it was my own client addressing the judge in this highly disrespectful manner. (Keep in mind that she is the one who wants something from the judge). A temperate and well-liked judge, I had never seen him angry—until that day, at my client. Not good. She wound up faring poorly the next week. While judges aren't supposed to hold poor behavior against people, they will weigh the credibility of your testimony based upon what they observe, so be respectful.

AT TRIAL

The lawyers will give their opening statements and then the petitioner (whoever filed the divorce case) will usually present their case first. That side will call all of their witnesses and ask them questions directly (direct examination). As each direct examination is completed, the other side will get to cross-examine that witness in an attempt to discredit the testimony or to bring out more information. The first lawyer gets one more shot to ask questions on re-direct. During these periods of questioning, the lawyer doing the direct examinations will present evidence and ask the judge to accept certain items as legal evidence. Also, the lawyers will object to a line of questioning or evidence based on various rules of law.

When the first side has finished calling their witnesses, the other side gets to present their case, call witnesses and present evidence. You will likely be called as a witness in your part of the case, and sometimes, the other lawyer might call you as a witness for the other side. As each witness testifies, you can make notes and pass them to your lawyer. This is especially helpful when you can remind your lawyer of various facts or fill in important background you have not covered.

When both sides are finished, the lawyers will make their closing arguments. Don't be surprised if you run out of time and the judge asks the lawyers to submit their closing arguments in writing.

If you finish everything, the judge may rule straight from the bench. More likely, especially if there are a lot of issues that need to be considered, the judge might take it under advisement. This means the judge wants time to read the memos of law, review the exhibits, and consider the testimony and arguments before rendering a ruling. Rulings can be written and mailed directly to your attorney. Or, on some occasions, the judge will make an oral pronouncement and direct the parties and lawyers to appear before the bench in order to making the ruling to you directly. The time lapse between trial and a ruling can seem like an eternity. Judges are busy and rulings can take a long time. It is definitely frustrating for both parties, but harassing the judge for a decision is not prudent.

If you don't like the ruling, your lawyer can ask the judge to reconsider or you can appeal it. Both of these actions carry stringent timelines. Often, if you don't file on time, you will be barred from having any further conversations about the ruling. If you appeal the decision, the appellate court can only decide if there was an error as a matter of law; no further evidence will be allowed. Appeals are very expensive and the win rate is pretty low, so weigh your decision to appeal carefully with the input of your attorney.

Day 35 Exercise

Choose your outfit for trial. Then take your journal and write all of the most important facts you think are essential to bring out to the judge. Write them down for your attorney. Set a date and time to meet with your attorney to practice your direct examination.

Day 35 Meditation/Affirmation

"No matter what events transpire today, I will remain calm. I can handle everything that comes my way with ease and grace."

Day 36

ESTATE PLANNING

What's more painful than the divorce process? The thought that your ex-spouse gets to decide whether or not to pull the plug on you if you are in a coma. Sometimes overlooked or forgotten, getting your estate plan updated is critical following a divorce.

Some states have laws that automatically terminate or revoke an ex-spouse's rights to your estate but some do not, and not all laws apply to every issue that needs to be addressed. Here is a short list of some things to think about after the divorce is final:

1. **For women:** If your maiden name has been restored, your first stop is the Social Security office to change your name with the Social Security Administration. You will need your divorce decree (or final judgment) and an official document that bears your maiden name (i.e., a birth certificate). Once you have changed it with the federal government, you can get a new driver's license and passport. Then address your bank account, credit cards, etc.

2. **Beneficiary designations:** Any asset which has a designated beneficiary, such as IRAs, life insurance policies, annuities and bank accounts, will go directly to that beneficiary. This occurs regardless of what your will or trust dictates. So if your ex-spouse is named as the beneficiary, and you no longer want your money to go to your former spouse if you die, change designations immediately.

3. **Will or trust:** Your will might designate your ex-spouse as the beneficiary and/or as the executor of your will. Your trust might also name your ex-spouse as the beneficiary of your trust assets, as well as the trustee of your trust. Choose someone else you trust to handle these matters. Financial institutions and/or estate planning attorneys also can be designated to handle the duties of executor or trustee.

4. **Power of attorney:** If your ex-spouse has power of attorney for you, it entitles your Ex to execute legal documents on your behalf. Designate a sibling, parent, child or close friend instead.

5. **Health care surrogate:** Yes, here we come to the plug pulling—and any other decisions to be made on your behalf if you are incapacitated. Definitely choose wisely here.

6. **HIPAA releases:** It is a good idea to sign these medical privacy waivers ahead of time for the people you want to grant access to your medical information. I once heard a horror story about a divorced woman who was hospitalized and was unconscious. Her only child, a daughter, was in the military in

Afghanistan and because there was no HIPAA (Health Insurance Portability and Accountability Act) release on file, she could not get information on the condition of her mother. After you sign these releases, give them to the parties to whom you are giving access so that they have it in the event it becomes necessary.

7. **Guardianship for minor children:** If something happens to you, your ex-spouse is likely to gain full custody of the children. You need to make arrangements for them, however, for the unlikely event that your spouse is unwilling or unable to care for them if something happens to you. Also, if you have minor children, make sure that trusts are set up for their benefit (the money doesn't go directly to them). The trustee of your children's trust will be the same person or people who will be the children's guardians.

A note about your final judgment or your marital settlement agreement: Make sure that you are taking steps to complete all transfers of ownership and other items provided in your agreement or final judgment. If you are to get the house, get the quit claim deed signed and recorded. Remove your spouse's name from your credit card immediately. Plan to complete transfers within 30 days. Also, make sure that you run a credit report a few months after the divorce to confirm that it is accurate.

For your estate plan changes, ideally you would contact an attorney to draft the documents. A local attorney knows the specifics of the law in your state and can ask questions that apply to you individually to ensure your estate plan comports with your specific needs. If you can't afford an attorney, there are several legal software programs and books available with do-it-yourself forms.

Getting your estate plan in order is an important step toward creating your new life, bringing you peace of mind, and declaring your freedom.

Day 36 Exercise

Review the checklist above. In your journal, make a list of the items you need to address. Decide that you will have it all completed within 30 days of the entry of your final divorce decree.

Day 36 Meditation/Affirmation

"Taking goal-directed actions is increasing my motivation to create my new life."

Day 37

FINANCIAL PLANNING

"*It's cheaper to keep her.*" These were the heartwarming words spoken by loving husband, Steve, before his wife of 30 years, Anna, found the Victoria's Secret receipt in his car for lingerie she curiously never saw. After the expensive battles and the costly war, they were finally divorced. She ended up with half the assets and a sizeable amount of permanent alimony. Steve might have been right, but the flaw in his financial strategy was that he didn't foresee that Anna might not want to keep him!

The financial impact of divorce on both men and women is staggering. According to statistics compiled by Utah State University, divorcees need an additional 30 percent in income to maintain the standard of living established during the marriage. To be sure, there is a financial impact on both men and women, but the financial effect of divorce on women, on average, is worse. One in five women, especially single mothers, fall below the poverty level after divorce. The average cost of divorce, including legal fees, income tax effects and other costs is estimated to range from $18,000 to $25,000 per individual.

As we have discussed, financial planning in divorce begins as soon as you realize that the divorce is imminent and it continues throughout the divorce process. Once the divorce is final, as physically and mentally drained as you might be, there are a few critical steps you need to take immediately:

1. **Determine your streams of income:** If you are receiving or paying alimony, expect tax ramifications. Unless the final judgment or marital settlement agreement specifically states that the alimony is not taxable to the payee and not deductible by the payor, then it is. If you are paying alimony, you will receive a tax deduction on that amount. If you are receiving alimony, you will have to pay income tax on that amount.

Plan for it.

Are you receiving child support or alimony? If so, for how long? Think about the term you will be receiving this support. If you will not be receiving support payments for a long period of time, form a strategy to replace that income as soon as you can.

Will you be receiving income from your investments? If so, make sure you hire a good financial advisor who will be conservative with your assets. Ask your advisor what a reasonable rate of return will be so you can plan for that income. Have a conversation with your financial advisor about how your portfolio is invested. If it is entirely invested so that you receive income, you will see very little growth. In the long term, you do want your portfolio to grow, so diversifying your portfolio may be a good idea. The types of assets you choose depend on your age, income, risk tolerance and the amount you are able to invest.

What is your earned income? Include guaranteed bonuses, and if you receive them regularly, earmark the bonuses for a particular use. For example, your budget should include gifts. If you receive your bonus in November, then earmark the bonus to pay for holiday gifts.

Do you need to get a job to generate more income? Do you need to go back to school to acquire new skills? If so, create a plan for how you will do that.

Will you be paying or receiving child support? Child support is not taxable to the payee and not deductible for the payor. The marital settlement agreement or final judgment of dissolution of marriage delineates the specific payment amount.

2. **Create a budget:** You should have already done this, but if you haven't, now is the time. Determine what your living expenses are, including your vacations. There are several online programs, such as mint.com, that can help you create a budget and monitor expenses within that budget. Make sure to include a savings component. Create a plan to pay off debts as soon as possible.

3. **Close joint credit cards and joint bank accounts:** Make sure that you close these accounts and start new ones to ensure that there is no confusion should an issue arise. If your spouse is responsible for a particular debt, make sure that there is a provision in your final judgment or marital settlement agreement which states that your spouse will hold you harmless from any responsibility associated with that debt, and if you pay it (to preserve your own credit score) then your spouse will indemnify you. Again, check your credit record in a few months to be sure that it is an accurate reflection of your financial picture.

4. **Complete transfers of assets:** If one spouse is receiving a piece of real estate, get the quit claim deed signed and recorded. Most states have waivers for transfer fees if the transfer is being done because of divorce. If you have retirement accounts that are being split, they may or may not require a Qualified Domestic Relations Order (QDRO) to effectuate the split. Regardless of whether a QDRO is necessary, make sure the person receiving a portion of the retirement account opens a new qualified account. A financial advisor can simply roll the portion into that account without creating a taxable event and without any penalties. Be aware of capital gains issues. If the assets held in the retirement accounts have had significant gains, then consider rolling the assets over "in kind" (without liquidating them into cash).

If your divorce includes the splitting of a pension, or monthly retirement payments being paid by one spouse's employer, then make sure that the company properly splits the benefit. Usually split pursuant to a QDRO, once the pension has been split, it becomes separate property for each spouse. Check with the company and your QDRO preparer to confirm the details of how and when it will be paid to each spouse.

5. **Check into Social Security income:** Under certain circumstances, you may qualify for benefits as a divorced spouse on a former spouse's Social Security record if:

- You were married to the former spouse for at least 10 years;
- You are at least 62 year of age;
- You are unmarried;

- You are not entitled to higher Social Security benefit on your own record.

There are some other requirements that apply if your former spouse is eligible to receive benefits. However, if your former spouse is eligible to receive benefits but has elected not to receive them, it does not preclude you from applying for the benefits as long you have been divorced for at least two years.

Consult with a Social Security Administration representative to become fully informed if you think you may qualify.

6. **Evaluate your insurance needs:** Major transition periods, such as following divorce, are an excellent time to reevaluate your insurance needs. Do you have adequate life, health, disability and home insurance? A certified financial planner, who is qualified to create a comprehensive financial plan tailored specifically to your needs, can help you assess your specific needs.

Day 37 Exercise

Go through Items 1-6 and create a to-do list. Next to each item, specify a completion date. Pull out your appointment calendar (on your phone or your date book). Put each item on your to-do list on your calendar. If you are using an electronic calendar, set it up to receive a reminder. Make sure the item is completed on the date and time you have specified.

Day 37 Meditation/Affirmation

"I am creating a plan for prosperity and am grateful for the abundance in my life."

Day 38

HEALTH

"*Emma Rae, I have a cookbook to put out*, and a daughter to raise, and the God damn winter Grand Prix, and I just don't have time for the nervous breakdown I so richly deserve, so please, don't ask me to stop and think!"—Julia Roberts as Grace in *Something to Talk About*

Divorce is traumatic and stressful. Some say it is the second-worst event one can experience (the worst being death)—others actually say it stands squarely at No. 1. In *Something to Talk About*, Julia Roberts' character is divorcing her philandering husband and she articulates that she is so overwhelmed with everything she has to do that she doesn't even have time to schedule a nervous breakdown.

The physical manifestations of stress on your body are uncontroverted. According to the medical website webmd.com, 43 percent of all adults suffer from some adverse effect of stress, and 75 percent to 90 percent of doctor's office visits are for stress-related ailments. Here are some of the ways that stress can manifest itself in your body:

- Depression

- Anxiety
- Weight loss
- Weight gain
- Lack of sleep/exhaustion
- Malnutrition
- Dehydration
- Headaches
- Nausea
- Joint pain
- Muscular issues
- Gastrointestinal issues
- Heart attacks or chest pain
- Ulcers
- Rashes and other skin issues
- Hair loss
- High blood Pressure

Take control of your life. Think clearly, act rationally and make sound decisions—decisions that will affect you and your family financially and emotionally for years to come. How can you do this? The only way is to take care of yourself throughout the entire process of divorce. With that mind, here are a few ideas:

GET AT LEAST 6-8 HOURS OF SLEEP EACH NIGHT

Sleep is more than just a restoration of energy. Studies show that a lack of sleep can lead to weight gain, accidents and injuries. It can also lead to heart attacks, strokes and diabetes. It adds to depression, lack of energy and irritability. If these reasons aren't enough, a lack of sleep can age your skin faster, and who wants that? For goodness sake, get enough sleep.

EXERCISE AT LEAST 3 TIMES A WEEK FOR 30 MINUTES

Even if you just walk the dog around the block for 30 minutes three times a week, your body will feel the effects of the extra oxygen and fresh air. Exercise releases endorphins, which elevate your mood. It also releases hormones that nourish the growth of brain cells.

TAKE VITAMIN SUPPLEMENTS

It is not possible to get all of the vitamins your body needs through the food you eat. Taking a multivitamin tailored to your age and lifestyle should become part of your daily regimen. Doctors can perform an analysis of your blood to determine which vitamins or minerals you are deficient in. Having inadequate levels of certain vitamins and minerals in your body can lead to a slower metabolism, sluggishness, hair loss and affect memory and concentration.

EAT HEALTHILY

It sounds cliché but you are what you eat. Personal trainer Jillian Michaels has talked about eating real food (not junk food). Try eating organic for a week or two to see if you feel better. If you are not sure which organic foods are the best to purchase then research "The Dirty Dozen" and "The Clean Fifteen" lists, which inform consumers which foods are laden with pesticides and which have the least.

RENEW OR REINVENT

I joke that right after a divorce, men get their teeth done (whitened or veneers) and women get their breasts enhanced. While these may or may not be options for you, this is a great time for renewing your fun side or inventing a new version of yourself. Try a different hairstyle, new fashions, or get a makeover.

LAUGH (OFTEN)

This one is so important that a whole chapter of this book is devoted to it. See Day 40.

SOCIALIZE

You might not feel like being around people, or think you are not good company, but you will feel more energized and positive if you socialize.

MEDITATE

Centering yourself and creating time to clear your mind is amazing therapy. Start with 30 seconds a day. Do it for a week, then work up to a minute. Eventually, try to meditate for at least 15 minutes day.

MANTRAS/AFFIRMATIONS

Having a mantra or affirmation that you state throughout the day helps to refocus your mind away from the negative thoughts that can flood your mind and replace them with positive ones.

SUPPORT GROUPS

Being with others who have been through what you are experiencing and seeing that people can live through it and create new lives will help you find coping strategies and inspiration.

PRIORITIZE

Don't get overwhelmed by the tasks that lie ahead. Prioritize what you have to do today, this hour, this minute. By focusing on priorities, you will feel more in control.

Day 38 Exercise

Consider the ideas for taking care of yourself. Choose a few that you can start immediately. Put them into your calendar and do them.

Day 38 Meditation/Affirmation

"I am healthy and fit and take care of my body."

Section Three

Spiritual FREEDOM

Day 39

FORGIVENESS

"The weak can never forgive. Forgiveness is an attribute of the strong."

– *Mahatma Gandhi*

When Gandhi proclaimed those words, he meant that it takes a certain inner strength and wisdom to see the benefits of forgiveness. The bells of freedom only ring for those who can learn to forgive; in fact, forgiveness is the path to freedom.

THE GREAT MYTH OF FORGIVENESS

The natural reaction to forgiving someone who has trespassed against you is that the person is "getting away" with an egregious act that's causing the need for forgiveness. If the offending party remains unforgiven, is justice truly served? The Great Myth of Forgiveness is that one has something to do with the other—that the offender and forgiveness and justice are rolled into one. But the truth is that forgiveness is a process within you: your mind, your heart and your soul.

There are two forms of forgiveness. The first is forgiving others.

Naomi was a bright 40-year-old attorney with a successful career when she met another smart attorney named Harry, also 40, and who had a bustling career. They began dating, and within a few months, she unexpectedly became pregnant. Both childless, they were reeling from the shock but were also ecstatic about having a child. About each other? Well, not so much. Naomi was crazy about Harry. Harry was crazy about himself. Despite the issues, Harry and Naomi walked down the aisle when she was seven months pregnant and they settled into their life together.

After their son was born, Naomi's life changed drastically. She made the decision to quit her position with the firm and stay home to care for the baby. Harry's life wasn't dramatically altered. He continued to work hard and play hard. While Naomi's days were filled with diapers, feedings and Mommy & Me gatherings, Harry went from work to tennis or golf, and nights out with the guys. Naomi's nagging pushed Harry further away. Eventually, the strain of the tension became unbearable, and when their son was 3 years old, Harry moved back to his bachelor pad.

The divorce, best described as acrimonious, was a protracted and painful process that took two years and many infusions of cash into their respective lawyers' accounts. After the separation, Harry looked only forward and not back, and he found comfort in the arms of other women. For years after the divorce, going to lunch with Naomi meant a one-sided conversation with Harry the Horrible. Naomi obsessed over what a selfish, ego-centric, manipulative, cold bastard Harry was. Harry, on the other hand, spent his days and nights working, playing golf, dating women and living the way he wanted. Would Naomi's forgiveness mean anything to him or affect his life? Not at all. On the other hand, what would Naomi's forgiveness do for Naomi?

One day, a friend of Naomi's pulled her aside and spoke to her about forgiveness. Initially, Naomi said she would never forgive him because he didn't deserve it. Her friend explained to her that forgiveness was for her, not for Harry; otherwise, she was allowing the poison of bitterness and resentment to course through her veins. The antidote to the poison of bitterness and resentment is forgiveness.

The second type of forgiveness can be more complicated: forgiving yourself. Anthony had been unfaithful to his first wife. Before she found out about it, he confessed then filed for divorce because he felt an overwhelming sense of guilt. After the divorce, he remarried but was unfaithful to his second wife. When he confessed to his second wife, she forgave him and expressed her desire to work on the marriage. Skeptical, he questioned how she could forgive him. That was her choice. His choice was to decide if he wanted to keep dragging his past into his future or leave the past in the past.

Forgiveness is letting go. Let go of the past because it no longer exists. The future is uncertain. The only thing that actually exists is this moment. Choose to live free from anger and hatred. Many are under the impression that forgiveness is a long process filled with anguish. The opposite can be true. Forgiveness is a gift that makes you feel lighter and creates an opening for joy that was not present before.

American humorist Mark Twain summed it up the best when he said, "Forgiveness is the fragrance that the violet sheds on the heel that has crushed it."

Day 39 Exercise

1. What has your ex-spouse done to offend, anger or hurt you? Write it down.

2. As you review the list, imagine you are talking to your ex-spouse. Say to them, "I forgive you. I forgive you for_____(list each offense). I now release you. You are free and I am free."

3. Take a deep breath. Notice how much lighter you feel. Smile. Take a moment of gratitude for this opportunity to be free.

Day 39 Meditation/Affirmation

"I am liberated as I release the past to the universe."

Day 40

LAUGHTER

"*I married Miss Right.* I just didn't know her first name was Always."
— *Unknown*
"My mother always said don't marry for money; divorce for money."
—*Wendy Liebman*
"Ah yes, divorce, from the Latin word meaning to rip out a man's genitals through his wallet." – *Robin Williams*

While these little quips are a bit jaded, they are humorous observations about the divorce process. As you well know, the process of divorce is excruciating and this is a critical time for you to find some levity.

"Laughter is the best medicine" is a classic maxim backed by science. Laughter really is good for your health. In fact, the field of gelotology (from the Greek word "gelos" meaning laughter) is the study of the psychological and physiological benefits of laughter. The benefits are so strong that psychologists prescribe "laughter therapy" and yogis have developed "laughter yoga" and "laughter meditation".

These are some ways that laughter is good for your health:

- Relives tension and allows the body to relax
- Lowers blood pressure
- Releases mood-lifting endorphins and dopamine
- Reduces stress hormones, such as cortisol
- Exercises the muscles in your abdomen and diaphragm
- Burns calories
- Increases your oxygen level, which stimulates your organs and increases your circulation
- Releases neuropeptides, which help fight strees and disease
- Boosts your immune system by activating T-cells in your body
- Allows you to connect and bond with others
- Enhences your mood and provides a general sense of well-being
- Reduces depression and increases feelings of hope, positivity and joy

    Human beings are unique from other species in our gift of laughter. Statistics show that on average, children laugh 400 times a day. Adults only laugh about 11 times a day, and sometimes less. Stanford University Medical School psychotherapist Dr. William Fry has researched the benefits of laughter and says that in addition to the benefits listed above, it is a great workout. Laughing 100 times a day, he says, is the cardiovascular equivalent of rowing for 10 minutes. Laughing sounds like more fun than rowing.

Laughter is a universal language. Just as Uncle Albert sings "I Love to Laugh" in Mary Poppins, we all love to laugh. More than just the psychological or physiological benefits, laughter is food for your soul. It is the path to spiraling upward instead of downward. During and after a divorce is an opportune time to cultivate a habit of laughter.

Day 40 Exercise

Make a list of the things that make you laugh.

Choose a few things to do from this list:

1. Collect cartoons and funny pictures or sayings that make you laugh. Post them where you will see them during daily routines (bathroom mirror, work desk, refrigerator).
2. Record clips of comedians who make you laugh. For the longest time, I had a clip of Eddie Murphy's "Ice Cream Man" skit on my iPod. Very funny.
3. Spend time with people who make you laugh or bring out the comedian in you.
4. Watch a comedy. If a few really make you laugh, buy the DVD and watch them again and again.
5. Schedule an evening at a local comedy club.

Day 40 Meditation/Affirmation

"I am cultivating a habit of laughter by bringing it into my life every day."

Day 41

DECLARATION

A declaration is more than a powerful statement. It is the first step in creation. Much of what has come into existence began with a declaration. When Orville and Wilbur Wright declared that they were going to invent a contraption that would fly humans through the sky, no one thought it was possible because it had never been done. When Thomas Jefferson, John Adams, Benjamin Franklin and their contemporaries declared it was time to establish a new nation, they were viewed as treasonous renegades. If a few guys got together today and said, "We are going to start our own country," would you take them seriously?

On Day 12, we talked about *The Four Agreements* and the power of word to create story. We can harness the power of word just as easily to create anything we want through our declarations. Just as our Founding Fathers declared their independence, you can declare your own independence.

In one of his public television presentations, Dr. Wayne Dyer talks about the power of the words "I Am." He explains that beginning in childhood, there is a conditioning of our minds in the realm of "I am not." Our self-talk is often unkind. If self-talk had a name it would have "Bully" in it. We often find ourselves saying things to ourselves like "I am not smart enough," "I am fat," "I am not pretty enough," "I am not strong enough," "I am not likeable" and the poisonous list goes on. Eventually, we start to believe this voice and see evidence of it in reality. Then it's justified: "See! My self-talk (a/k/a Bully) is right!" Like trick mirrors, this is one of the tricks that bullying self-talk plays on you. In reality, the evidence doesn't come first and then you think it. The truth is that *it is actually the other way around*. First, your mind thinks it, *then* you begin "seeing it" in your world.

History is replete with highly-evolved souls who have known this truth and have spoken it. "The mind is everything. What you think you become," Buddha extolled. Psychologists have called it a "self-fulfilling prophecy." From a purely physical stance, your thoughts are energy. When a thought forms in the brain, it ignites physical and biological waves of energy that are emitted into the world. Just as you can feel the warmth of a fire—even though you can't see the warmth—you know the warmth is there because you can feel it. While you can't feel the warmth of your thoughts or see them emitting energy, they are sending messages out into the universe and into your world. Your thoughts set up your world to match accordingly. It is a mirror that reflects back to you, not the other way around. Once you realize this, you begin to understand that it is not possible for your world to be created in any other way other than the way you have ordered it through your thoughts.

If you decide that your world is chaotic, you are a poor money manager, you are drawn to the wrong type of people, and you fail at relationships, your thoughts will set about creating that reality for you. Your thoughts are like little worker elves who run out into the world upon your command and do as you have instructed. They know nothing else than to carry out the wishes of their master. You cannot hold on to these negative ideas and magically become highly organized, a great investor or the right mate with the ideal person. Just simply not possible.

When you make a declaration, don't use qualifiers such as "I hope" or "maybe" or "I will try." A declaration is a commanding statement made with complete conviction. Your worker elves don't understand qualifying words; they only understand commands. Dr. Martin Luther King, Jr. understood the power of declaration when he delivered his celebrated "I Have a Dream" speech. He stood up in front of millions of people and declared his dream. His speech would not have had the same impact if he said, "I have a dream that I hope that maybe someday people will judge my children on the content of their character, if they try, instead of the color of their skin, even though I doubt that is ever going to happen."

Words have power. Thoughts have power. They have this with or without you having an awareness of it, but you have complete control once you are aware of it. In divorce, the insidious orders handed to your worker elves might sound like this:

"My husband is very good at manipulating everybody. He is smarter than everyone and he always wins, so I will never get what I want."

"My wife is so stubborn that she will never agree to a reasonable alimony."

"I always pick the wrong person. No matter what, they always cheat on me and are abusive to me."

Decide today that you will harness your power and declare your independence for the rest of your life. One of my all-time favorite quotes is from *Star Wars: The Empire Strikes Back*. In a pivotal scene, Yoda is training a young Master Luke Skywalker to become a Jedi. When Luke says, "All right, I'll give it a try," Yoda responds, "Try not. Do or do not. There is no try." When you say "I'll try" or "I hope," you might as well say "This is going to fail." The result is the same. In order for your declarations to have power, they must override the thoughts that have worn grooves into your mind. Those old grooves must be destroyed so that new ones can be built. Your worker elves have grown accustomed to their old set of orders. You have to remind them constantly that their old orders are no longer in the playbook.

Declarations are not goals. Aspirational in nature, goals may or may not be attained. Aspirations may or may not be realized. A declaration is a command to your world that, "This is how it is." Period. When you say, "I am a human being," you are sure that you are a human being. You don't think, "Well, maybe I am a lion." You know it with every cell in your body. Your declarations are no different. Once you declare them, you have to know that they are real and true with every fiber of your being. Anything less and they have no power. If you want a different life, declare it. Feel it. Know it.

Day 41 Exercise

It is time to declare what you want.

1. Take your journal and write out the following categories: Personal Declarations, Career Declarations, Relationship Declarations, Financial Declarations, Spiritual Declarations.
2. Write five declarations under each category. Start with commands like "I am," "I declare" and "It is"— written in the present tense. Make sure your worker elves know exactly what they are being sent out to do for you.
3. Read your declarations every day. Know that they are real as you say them. Memorize them and remind yourself of them several times throughout the day. See the changes in your reality start to take place.

Day 41 Meditation/Affirmation

"I am declaring that my life is exactly as I want it to be."

Day 42

INTEGRITY

When *I was in sixth grade*, my teacher, Mrs. Shea, gave me my first lesson about integrity. One day, we were supposed to have a nerve-wracking test. Throughout the day, we kept thinking it was coming. By lunch, still no test. The minutes clicked by and she didn't bring it up, so neither did we. At 3 p.m., the bell rang, and we were dismissed! We sprang up and bolted toward the door, with no mention of the test.

The next morning, we quietly filed in, again with no plans to mention the test. When we took our seats, Mrs. Shea quietly glided to the front of the class completely silent. We remained uncomfortably silent as she picked up the chalk and began to write on the blackboard. She wrote one word in capital letters: INTEGRITY. She proceeded to define it for us. "Integrity is having high moral values and ethics," she explained. We took the test that day and got a dose of punishment along with it for good measure. Lesson learned.

Integrity does mean to adhere to a high standard of honesty, morals and values. It also means that something is structurally sound. It comes from the Latin word *"integer"* which means being whole or complete, so integrity is the foundation upon which we build our lives. In fact, I will suggest to you that without integrity, nothing in your life will work. Just as tendons and ligaments hold together your bones and muscles, integrity holds everything together in your life.

In virtually every area of your life, the opportunity to choose to operate with or without integrity is present. Integrity is making a choice to do the right thing, to honor your word to others and to yourself, and to operate at your highest level of being. Choosing not to operate within the context of integrity is a choice to cheat others—that is clear. What is not readily apparent is that operating outside of the context of integrity is choosing to cheat *yourself*. While the effects may or may not appear immediately, they always appear. Often, because there is a time lapse, people begin to blame others because of the lack of workability in their personal lives, their workplace, and their finances.

Building your life upon a foundation that lacks integrity is the equivalent to the two little pigs who built their houses out of straw or sticks. One huff and one puff, and it will come crashing down. Creating a life with integrity is building the brick house that the third little pig built. No amount of huffing and puffing from any big bad wolves will blow it over. Recently, I saw Lance Armstrong being interviewed on *Oprah*. As he recounted the web of lies he had carefully spun for many years, I thought about how his life had been built without the benefit of the most important ingredient: integrity. Like the straw house, everything he worked for came crashing down. He lost his reputation, accolades and endorsement contracts. His decision to operate with a lack of integrity came with tremendous personal and professional cost.

Integrity means doing the right thing, even when no one else is watching and no one will ever find out. Like the principle in physics —for every action, there is an equal and opposite reaction—your actions will cause reactions. If you have acted in an unethical or dishonest manner, the opposite reaction will not be pleasant. My father always used to caution us, "Be careful what you throw into the air. It is liable to come back down and hit you in the head." Choosing not to honor your word or to be dishonest is a choice against yourself.

In Day 41, Declaration, we discussed the importance of declaring who you are and what your life looks like. We are the alchemists of our lives, creating our world the way we want it to be by commanding it to be so. Our declarations are the bones and muscles and integrity is the ligaments and tendons. In order for the bones and muscles to operate together as a unit, the ligaments and tendons have to pull them together. In order for our declarations to become reality, there must be a system of integrity.

Here is how it works—or more aptly, doesn't work. Let's say that you have declared that you are whole and complete and that you interact with people as though they are whole and complete. You meditate on it in the morning, carry it in your car, read a pop-up reminder on your phone, and have posted it on your office computer. Then one day, you spend an hour telling your spouse what a jackass he is and delve into specific details about his various shortcomings. Is this interacting with your spouse as if he is whole and complete? Clearly not. This is an excellent example of how you are making him wrong and you right. Interacting with others as though they are whole and complete is not making anyone wrong.

Therefore, once you have made your declarations, you must have the integrity to stick to them. Otherwise, you are *out of integrity*. You are not honoring your word. Your words have awesome power. Respect the power of your words by knowing that once you declare something, it is. If you have declared that you are strong and confident, then feelings of insecurity are not who you are. Those feelings are felt by who you once were. You are strong and confident, and if you aren't, then you are out of integrity. Without integrity, nothing in your life will work. With it, your life will be exactly as you declare that it is.

Day 42 Exercise

Each day as you state your declarations, look for ways that you might be out of integrity. If you recognize that you are out of integrity, clean it up. If you need to speak to someone to let them know that you have not kept your word, do that. Own up to your responsibilities. If you have said you have promised you were going to do something by a certain time, and you haven't kept your word, own up to that. By cleaning up your integrity, you make yourself whole again. Do this each and every day. We will not always operate within integrity but we can always navigate the ship back on course by taking control of the wheel.

Day 42 Meditation/Affirmation

"I operate at the highest level of integrity with my family, my friends, my colleagues and everyone with whom I interact."

Day 43

PASSION

While standing in line at the grocery store, you have probably noticed that many magazines have some version of an article about how to live your passion. Finding your passion has become a national pastime, though how many of us have really found it? If you have, how much time do you spend pursuing it? Some of us are still on the quest. What is passion anyway? Passion is defined as a strong and barely controllable emotion or a state or outburst of such emotion. More to the point, if your declarations are like bones and muscles, and integrity like tendons and ligaments, passion is the energy that propels the body.

WHAT WOULD YOU DO IF YOU KNEW YOU COULDN'T FAIL?

A few years ago, I heard someone posit the question, "What would you do if you knew you couldn't fail?" The answer to that question might have something to do with your passion. So often, we make a decision that a particular outcome is not attainable before we even start it. Your internal conversation might sound like this, "I could never get that job. They want someone with certain qualifications that I don't have." So you don't apply, and somehow they don't choose you for the job! Oh, that's right: You can't get a job for which you didn't apply. Yet, if you knew you couldn't fail, you would have applied for it.

THE PASSION BEFORE THE PASSION

As you create your new life, you should discover or rediscover your passion. I once heard Will Smith in an interview with Barbara Walters respond to a question as to whether or not he would ever run for president of the United States. He laughed, then became serious. To paraphrase, he replied, "No, I do not plan to run for president. But I will tell you this. If I wanted to be the president. I. Would. Be. The. President." Will Smith is currently one of the most powerful men in Hollywood. How did he get there? Unwavering passion about who he is, what he believes in, and everything that he does.

Passion is more than just feeling positive about something. It is more than being enthusiastic about an activity. Passion consumes you. It is something you feel with every cell in your body, as well as your heart, your mind and your spirit. It is what you would do without being paid. It is what you feel you have to do. It keeps coming up in your thoughts even while you're engaged in other activities.

So many of us don't even know what we love to do, which makes talk of passion confounding and frustrating. We hear talk show hosts touting it, we read the magazine articles and the blogs, but this life filled with passion seems to evade us. Sometimes, we have spent so many years working, caring for our families, and doing what we *have* to do, it hasn't even occurred to us to consider what we *love* to do. Or we view it as a luxury that we won't allow ourselves to indulge.

If I am describing you, then it is time to indulge. But before we get to that—here's a rub you might not have expected—you actually have to have passion about finding your passion. Sound ironic? Maybe. But if you are so apathetic at this point that you don't care about finding your passion, then you will remain stuck where you are. You have to want to move mountains. You have to decide that NOW is the time—that you've lived long enough without it and you will NOT stand for that. You are going to take control right here, right now and begin living your life to the fullest. You deserve it. Your family, friends and co-workers will be better served because you will be light, ebullient and brimming with life.

LIVING YOUR PASSION

The first step to living your passion is to live passionately. Overcoming your own inertia is the first step. Thinking about things, then not following through, does not bring change. Maybe you had heard the saying, "If you keep doing what you're doing, you're going to keep getting what you're getting." Seems so common sense but very true. If you don't inject some enthusiasm for what you are doing right now, you will not see any change. If you are not sure how to do that, Alexandra Stoddard offers more than 500 ways to infuse joy into daily life in her book "Living a Beautiful Life." Her suggestions include lighting a candle and listening to beautiful music while paying your bills, adding fresh flowers to your evening dinner table, or throwing cumin into a soup you have eaten 100 times before. By beginning to feel passionate, you will begin to feel more creative and more alive. As that happens, you will begin to notice that you are excited about things you may have never noticed before. A zest for living will emerge.

The next step to living your passion is to surround yourself with others who have a passion for life. Join a book club or take a ballroom dance class. If you have always wanted to learn to race a car, spend a week at a racing school. If you have always wanted to learn how to fish or play tennis, now is the time. Sign up for a lesson. If you like it, take another or join a club. Get your friends involved.

The third step is to schedule time, at least an hour each week, to devote to your interests. Put it on the calendar. View that time slot just as if it were an appointment with your most important client. Schedule around it. If something comes up, you are not available that evening. Protect it with vigilance.

The fourth step is to listen to your intuition. Once you have started to implement the previous steps, your passion will start to emerge. It will be that thing to which you can't wait to get. You will find yourself devouring every bit of information you can find on it. Your spare time will be spent Googling articles, buying books about it, and seeking out others who share this interest. You will be living it, and just as you require sleep and food to live, you will feel like you need this passion in your life to live.

The last step is creating a life around your passion. Start doing it every single day. Put passion behind each one of your declarations. Look for ways to incorporate them into everything you do. Start creating outcomes for your passion. Commit to the outcomes. Create a vision board. Write about it. Talk about it. Place all of your heart, soul and energy into living into your new reality every minute of every day.

Day 43 Exercise

Review the five steps to living your passion. Write down the ways that you are going to implement them. Write down five ways that you are going to start adding energy and vitality to your life today. At the end of the day, check them off. Keep reviewing until you are living a life in passion.

Day 43 Meditation/Affirmation

"I feel an intense flame of passion growing inside me and I am enthused about all of the possibilities."

Day 44

POWER

"Being powerful is like being a lady. *If you have to tell people you are, you aren't." – Margaret Thatcher.*

Several years ago, I attended a Halloween party with my boyfriend (who later became my husband). During the event, a gentleman approached me, stuck his hand out to shake mine, and he boastingly introduced himself with, "Hello. My name is Joe Lawyer, and I am a very prominent attorney in this town." That was not his real name obviously, but this is an absolutely true story. (Okay, I left out the part about my eye roll after his introduction.)

AUTHENTIC POWER

The world often defines power as having great wealth, a position of great exultation or dominion or control over others. Adolph Hitler had external power for several years; he controlled whole nations for a period of time. He played God when he decided who lived or died. That is not authentic power. In fact, even though he would have never admitted it, Hitler was a coward. He felt so little authentic power within that he desperately attempted to assuage his fears by gaining external power. As Margaret Thatcher observed, Hitler had to tell people he was powerful, and so did Joe Lawyer.

Authentic power is not competitive. It does not feel the need to be better, stronger, faster or smarter than another. It is not fed by controlling others or being judgmental, degrading or abusive. Authentically powerful people are not duplicitous, deceitful or hypocritical. The quest for external power leaves behind a feeling of emptiness. Inauthentic power is a vacuum, a black hole of insecurity. No sum of money and no high position can fill that void. Another person cannot fill that void either. Inauthentic power=hole. Authentic power=whole.

People who are authentically powerful source their power from within themselves. The source is deep within your core. Like an oak tree that stands firm in the wind, an authentically powerful person is secure in his or power regardless of surrounding chaos. Authentic power is steadfast. Nelson Mandela, Gandhi and the Dalai Lama are clear examples of authentically powerful people. In the book, *The Four Agreements*, one of the agreements you make with yourself is that you will never take anything personally. The reason for that is because the *way people treat other people is a direct reflection of the way they feel about themselves.* The way people treat others doesn't have anything to do with you. Authentic people treat others with respect and kindness.

By overcoming fear, you begin to feel your power. Think about the times in your life when you finally did something you were initially afraid to do. Maybe it was riding a twisting rollercoaster that you swore you would never get on. Once you got off, you felt a sense of accomplishment. By facing your fears head-on and overcoming them, you nurture your authentic power. Face them again and again and you will begin to feel stronger and more complete than you ever have.

Authentic power makes you feel worthy and peaceful. Authentically powerful people never worry that their star will lose brilliance when another person's star is shining. In fact, when you become authentically powerful, you realize that one star's light has nothing to do with the light of another one. When everyone shines, the world is illuminated.

Transitioning out of a relationship is scary and difficult. Realizing that you can smoothly do it in a way in which you feel whole and complete is an accomplishment. Overcoming your fears, worries and anger, and emerging stronger, more secure and more joyful than ever is a triumph.

CHOICE

In each moment of each day, you are given a gift: the gift of choice. You have the choice to reach higher toward your authentic power, your true self (who you have declared yourself to be and with your integrity continue to be). You also have the choice to allow yourself to be driven and controlled by your lower self (and your insecurities). You have the power to choose to leave your past behind and choose the future you want.

The basic scientific law known as cause and effect applies to our lives. Most of us live as an effect by claiming or making the excuse that we are who we are as a direct effect of everything that has happened to us in the past. Examples of "effect" statements are:

I am very shy because I was bullied as a child.

I have a temper because my parents were abusive to me.

I don't feel attractive because I was always told I was fat as a child.

I have no value because my spouse constantly puts me down.

I am insecure because my romantic partners are unfaithful to me.

These types of statements have no power. This type of thinking assumes that others have the power to choose your value or your worth. It falsely assumes that anyone else has anything to do with *your* worth or *your* power.

True power is in choosing to be the *cause* and not an *effect*. You get to declare that you are a powerful person. You are confident and secure. You know that you have intrinsic value. There is a redemptive power in knowing that you don't have to be an effect of what's happened to you. You can be the cause of any reality you choose to create, so decide that is what you are doing. Effect=powerless. Cause=powerful.

Day 44 Exercise

1. Be aware of what choices you are making today. Are you making a choice to reach toward your authentic self and be the cause in your world? Or are you making a choice to continue to be an effect and remain powerless? Write down each time you make one choice or the other.

2. Notice in each moment when you choose power how your circumstances change. Journal what you have observed.

3. Continue to do this until you begin to see a shift in your world.

Day 44 Meditation/Affirmation

"I AM POWERFUL!"

Day 45

FREE

I once heard a comedienne observe, "My husband no longer wants to be married. He said until death do us part. So I guess I am going to have to kill him." That's one way to be free. Well, until the authorities find you and send you to prison. That's not so free.

YOUR DECLARATION OF INDEPENDENCE

Being free has different contexts in the environment of divorce. Freedom means the absence of boundaries and limitations. The word divorce is derived from the Latin word *"divortere"* which means to divert. Divorce doesn't mean to dissolve or to sever; it means to diverge. It simply means that each person has moved in a different direction, each one free to choose how his or her new life will be created.

Freedom can mean being free from your marriage or free from being under the control of the other person's will. To some, freedom means being able to choose whatever television show they want to watch or buy whatever they want without having to consult with another person. In the sitcom *Seinfeld*, when the character George lost his fiancée, he proclaimed that summer to be the "Summer of

George." His bachelor paradise included sitting around his house stripped to the waist while eating a block of cheese the size of a car battery. Each of us has a different ideal about what being free means. Regardless of the specifics, so often people observe that they didn't realize how much they were putting up with until they didn't have to anymore—like that old adage about how when you stop banging your head against the wall, you realize how good it feels.

Independence is one aspect of freedom. Feeling free to express yourself and make your own choices is essential. Our Founding Fathers understood that completely when they decided to found an entire nation on that principle:

> When in the Course of human events, it becomes necessary for one people to dissolve the political bands which have connected them with another, and to assume among the powers of the earth, the separate and equal station to which the Laws of Nature and of Nature's God entitle them, a decent respect to the opinions of mankind requires that they should declare the causes which impel them to the separation.

As Thomas Jefferson so eloquently penned in the Declaration of Independence, it sometimes becomes necessary to dissolve the bands which have connected you to another, and assume the power given to you, and to which you are entitled by nature and God, to declare the reasons why you need to be separated.

THE SURPRISE FREEDOM

The real freedom you didn't expect to find after your divorce is liberation from your afflictions. While it appears elusive, this Lady

Liberty is actually easy to find. You just have to know where to look. By realizing that you are strong, you find freedom. By understanding that you are fearless, you find freedom. By recognizing that you have the power to declare who you are and what you want, you find freedom. By knowing with all your heart, your soul and every faculty that you are powerful beyond measure, you experience freedom.

Being set free from a relationship that does not serve your highest self is a gift. The surprise gift you didn't expect is the unearthing and unleashing of the hero that has always lived inside of you. The surprise is that it is in this process of transition and discovery, you begin to clear a space. By exorcising the demons of fear, worry, anger, resentment and bitterness, you make room for the possibilities of declaration, integrity, laughter, passion, power and freedom.

Another real surprise is that by learning these things and clearing that space, you also make room for allowing the possibility of a new relationship. Only this time, you will offer your new self, who is whole and complete, into the relationship. Instead of looking for another to fill your void, you will bring into your life another person who is also whole and complete.

Discovering every type of freedom is the silver lining in your divorce. This shift in perspective will be your true measure of freedom. Your time has come to shine your light upon the world. Let freedom ring!

Made in United States
Troutdale, OR
03/31/2024